BIRDS IN A CAGE

BIRDS IN A CAGE

DEREK NIEMANN

CB

First published in 2012 by Short Books
3A Exmouth House
Pine Street
EC1R 0JH

This paperback edition published in 2013

10 9 8 7 6 5 4 3 2 1

A CIP catalogue record for this book is available from the British Library.

ISBN 978-1-78072-136-1

Printed and bound in Great Britain by CPI Group (UK) Ltd, Croydon, CR0 4YY

Illustration and photo credits:

All bird illustrations by Rob Hume
p.viii Imperial War Museum
p.7 John Furdson
p.11, 26, 68, 126, 208, 212, 214, 216, 230 The Conder family
p.30, 114, 116 Scottish Ornithologists' Club
p.40 PF Haynes
p.48 H Harrington
p.50 WSA Clough-Taylor
p.77 AR Borrett
p.78 CH Stanford
p.130 Alexander Library of Ornithology
p.171,172 Jan & Tony Pickup
p.194 Sarah Niemann
p.286 Mike Richards (RSPB)
p.288 John Topham
p.290 Jas. MacGeoch and Dennis Coutts

Contents

INTRODUCTION

"Whilst being a prisoner of war was not a particularly recommended occupation, it was, for all but a few, better than being dead."
Peter John Conder, aimless schoolboy, reluctant advertising executive, Second Lieutenant Royal Corps of Signals, POW Number 346, Skokholm Island warden, director of the Royal Society for the Protection of Birds (RSPB)

Nearly six million men fought for Britain in the Second World War. Probably all considered the possibility that they might be wounded or killed. But an army psychologist discovered a remarkable fact: hardly any imagined they would be taken prisoner. It was a thought beyond contemplation; degrading, dispiriting captivity at the hands of the enemy for an indefinite period of time. That was too much for their minds to bear.

This book follows the stories of four men who overcame hunger, hardship, fear and stultifying boredom to bring purpose to their lives behind barbed wire. Through natural history, and especially birds, they regained self-respect and a passion for living. In the words of one, birds "occupied hundreds and hundreds of hours during which, in spirit, I was not confined."

Though up to five years of their young lives were stolen under imprisonment, they all returned home determined to make something of themselves. And they did.

Peter Conder became director of the RSPB, transforming it from a tiny amateurish club into an enduring force for nature conservation. George Waterston established Fair Isle as a bird observatory and became a founder of wildlife tourism when he established an osprey nestwatch at Loch Garten that would attract more than two million visitors and massive publicity over the following decades. John Buxton, the teacher of them all, wrote *The Redstart*, one of the most acclaimed and lyrical natural history books of the twentieth century, and left a legacy of profound and moving war poetry. And John Barrett acknowledged the debt that he owed natural history for providing solace in his darkest days by opening it up for millions to enjoy: arguably the inventor of the modern guided walk, and author of the century's most popular seashore guide, he taught and encouraged thousands.

These men found meaning among squalor and their enthusiasm and indomitable spirit inspired others in the POW camps. We hope their story inspires you.

THE CAST

Main Characters

Name: **Edward John Mawby Buxton**
Rank: **Second Lieutenant, 1st Independent Company**
Date and place of birth: **16th December 1912, Bramwell, Cheshire**
Education: **Malvern and New College, Oxford**

"Strongly built, darkly handsome and intelligent, sensitive to the point of seeming to have fewer skins than other men", John Buxton was gifted with three aces in his hand, yet always seemed to complain about not having been given a fourth. His father was a Lancashire cotton mill owner, his home a large mansion in Wilmslow, Cheshire, with a walled garden, greenhouses and stables. He travelled widely in Europe with his family, and his father encouraged him to pursue interests in birdwatching, literature and archaeology.

Packed off to Malvern School, Buxton scooped up prizes in English, Greek and Latin, displaying the formidable intelligence that would make him – as a friend later commented

– "always the cleverest person in the room". New College, Oxford followed, and he graduated in 1935 with a Masters degree in literature. He was already a brilliant student of literature, a poet, linguist, archaeologist and ornithologist. But what would he do next?

Buxton had one certainty about his future career: "I shall not go into business NEVER," he wrote to Christopher Cox, his former tutor at Oxford, thus incurring his father's displeasure. He told his parents that he would do whatever turned up for the next three years. Sure enough, for that allotted period, he searched for direction, revealing in his letters a tendency towards

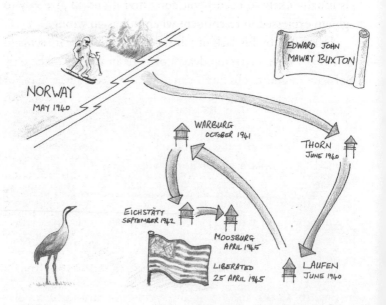

self-pity and unrelenting criticism of others. "I have refrained from plaguing you with my chronic state of unemployment for some time," he wrote to his tutor, after flunking an interview at the Victoria and Albert Museum. Two months later, he mused: "If I were to write or rather publish anything which was well-received I think my father would then be prepared to give me enough to be independent." After Buxton abandoned an archaeological dig in Palestine when it did not meet his expectations, Cox was trenchant in outlining the young man's shortcomings. "I'm sorry to preach but I do think that you have at present rather a tendency to expect perfection almost as a right and then not only to be disappointed but to be bitter when (as is usually likely to occur) you don't find it and to give way to gloom expressed in resentment when things go wrong."

Frustrated by his lack of job success at home – "It seems to me that I have a striking dearth of irons in the fire – the only jobs are museum jobs and I can't say there seem to be many of them" – Buxton went to Norway in 1937, where he spent his time teaching English to the king's aide-de-camp and gained some kind of maturity. In those months, Buxton discovered he had a gift for teaching. His Norwegian employer thought so too, inviting him to return for the following summer. Buxton departed for England in September 1937 and decided to take a natural history holiday for a few weeks on Skokholm, an island off the west coast of Wales. He quickly fell under the spell of one of the century's most influential naturalists.

The ornithologist-farmer tenant of Skokholm was one Ronald Lockley. Cardiff-born, Lockley had pursued a brief career as a poultry farmer, before having a Swiss Family Robinson moment when he decided romantic island life was for him. He had come to farm the island in 1927, also launching a venture to breed chinchilla rabbits. Though the animals failed to breed like bunnies, Lockley stayed on, supplementing his fishing and farming income with a sideline in writing lyrical books about the life of "the island naturalist" that brought a measure of fame in the outside world. Crucially, he also established Skokholm as Britain's first bird observatory. Lockley introduced the recently-invented Heligoland trap to the island, a funnel-net by means of which migrating birds could be caught, ringed and released unharmed. His own detailed studies centred on Manx shearwaters, puffins and petrels. The country's finest ornithologists, including Julian Huxley and Max Nicholson, flocked to Skokholm, and Buxton, always a quick learner, was to receive enough education from these illustrious figures during his stays there to last him a birdwatching lifetime.

During that first visit, Buxton appeared to find some release from his doubts. Lockley remembered an engaging, happy young man who carried the warden's own daughter around on his shoulders and impressed the more experienced naturalist with his knowledge and application. Lockley must have encouraged Buxton to return to Skokholm, for he did so in August of the following summer after another teaching stint in Norway.

Once more, he was to be captivated by a Lockley, but this time it was Ronald's sister Marjorie, who happened to be staying on the island. Theirs was a whirlwind, besotted romance. In a love letter to Marjorie, he wrote: "I tried so hard to make a poem for you... but I couldn't, for my words seem only like little paper boats; they cannot bear all my love or they must sink." There was an added sense of urgency to their courtship so typical of those uncertain days when young people rushed to live "in the now" before war came to blow away their future – Chamberlain had just returned from Munich with a doubtful promise of peace. Eight months after they first met, they married in April 1939 at Ovingdean Parish Church in Sussex.

Within a matter of weeks, the newly-wed couple was back on Skokholm. The Lockleys were planning to fly in May to

Buxton at the head of the wheelhouse table, Skokholm, 1939. His wife Marjorie is to his right. Buxton had taken temporary charge of the island while the Lockleys were studying shearwaters in the Atlantic.

Portugal, Madeira and other Atlantic islands to study the migration routes of shearwaters and petrels. The Buxtons were invited to stand in for them as wardens, running the observatory and carrying out studies of their own.

Lockley encouraged Buxton then – just as he would do two years later in a POW camp – to make a single species his own for intensive study. And just as he would do behind bars, Buxton chose a bird of beauty. For the next three months, he patiently and methodically recorded the behaviour of the island's 25 breeding pairs of oystercatchers. When the Lockleys returned in August, Buxton took the decision to submit his findings in a paper to the respected journal *British Birds*: "I had hoped to make this paper more complete by further observations; but in the present uncertain circumstances, I have thought it best to publish it now." Buxton showed it to his ornithological mentor for comment, then sent his paper off. War broke out only weeks later.

Name: **Peter John Conder**
Rank: **Second Lieutenant, 2nd London Regiment, Royal Corps of Signals**
Date and place of birth: **20th March 1919, London**
Education: **Cranleigh**

"Every day I go to a stuffy office to work in dust, dirt, stink and heat, and what is worse amid a desire for gaining 'filthy lucre'. I pray to heaven and nature to let me out of it and let me realise my ideal."

Two years before the gates of a POW camp would close behind him, Peter Conder was suffering a different kind of imprisonment. He had been born into a life of middle-class privilege; his father worked as a ship's broker in the City before joining his wife's family firm of SH Benson, Britain's first advertising agency. Yet Conder was a victim of his own inertia. His sister described him as "lazy": certainly he lacked academic motivation. Only one passion captivated this dreamy loner:

At the junior school set in fields I was encouraged by a master named Warre-Cornish to keep a bird diary which I did and at the end of the year, being the only boy who completed the diary – I won the prize which was a penknife. The only bird that I can remember from those days but which I did not identify until several years later, I remember calling on those long summer evenings, a continuous churring sound, almost mechanical. I heard it again several years later amongst the Scots pines and silver birches of Hurtwood. I was an older and more experienced birdwatcher (by then) and immediately realised it was a nightjar and remembered it singing ten years earlier.

At Cranleigh School, within sight of the South Downs, he belonged to the school ornithological society, but he was also beaten for birdwatching by masters frustrated at his lack of application in his school work. He left school without achievements or ambition and fell into the family firm for want of anything better. Within a year, he was bewailing "this endless drudgery of forced work in set hours. I hate it and the filthy, disgusting stink of horse dung and exhaust which fills the dirty grey streets of London". Weekend forays into the countryside, often sleeping out under the stars, only intensified his angst and

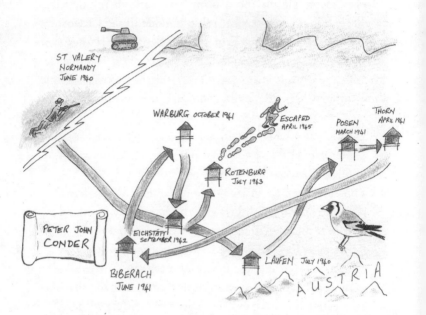

sense of alienation: "I must take more care every morning to watch and listen for these birds, for in my daily rush to work, I am beginning to lose my sense of observation." His diary from 1938 to 1939, a period during which his mother died, captures both his longing to escape from his London office, and self-awareness of his own debilitating inability to do anything to change his life: "I often think to myself that I shall never become a famous poet, writer, or naturalist because I take life too easily. I prefer rather than work at a book, to lounge in an armchair and listen to music."

*Second Lieutenant PJ Conder.
Photograph probably taken in
1939 prior to his departure for
France.*

Lounging was indeed a great passion. Friends recalled how Conder did not so much sit in a chair as ooze into it, with limbs sprawled out at all angles. He was an even-tempered, generally placid man, slow to anger. A telltale sign of Conder coming to boiling point was a tendency to whistle out of tune, "and when he called you 'chum' you knew you were in trouble".

Conder saw a way out of his passive frustration in the spring of 1939, when war was looking imminent. He enlisted in the Territorial Army and by June he was a professional soldier. The day before war broke out, he gained a commission as second lieutenant in the Royal Corps of Signals. On 4th December, with their initial training over, his unit embarked for northern France.

Name: **John Henry Barrett**
Rank: **Squadron Leader, 35 Squadron**
Date and place of birth: **21st July 1913, King's Lynn**
Education: Repton and **St John's College, Cambridge**

It was hard to ignore John Barrett. He stood well above most
of his contemporaries and had what a good friend called "the
loudest voice of anyone I ever met. He had a very emphatic
way of speaking, and the way he expressed himself (with
great use of his facial muscles) was quite impressive. I suppose
he was acting a part and thoroughly enjoying it. He had a
curious personal tic, using his forefinger, at right angles to

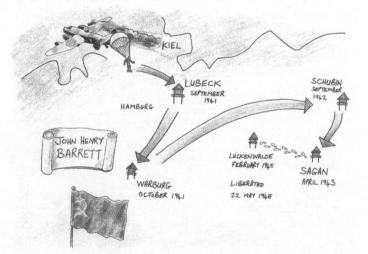

his scalp, to wind up his forelock into a spiral. He was a dominant, but not domineering personality".

John Henry Barrett nevertheless bent to the wills of others at critical moments during the first 27 years of his life. He came from an affluent background. Though his father had been killed in the Second Battle of Ypres when he was only four years old, Barrett's extended Norfolk family would always be on hand to support him.

Barrett described his childhood self as "blankly ignorant, unguided and quite uninspired". He was about seventeen years old when the family moved to Orchard Lodge in Cringleford, a village on the outskirts of Norwich. "Until we reached the Lodge I do not recall that I ever paid attention or listened to the birds, butterflies and wild flowers that I now had around me. The previous gardens had been no more than suburban rectangles. Now I must have fallen into new ways. The birds particularly... the beauty, the variety, the wonder began to possess me. I read all I could find."

The now passionate naturalist gained first-class training from Ted Ellis, the patient and inspiring curator at the Castle Museum, and his uncle Henry, the first treasurer of the newly formed Norfolk Naturalists' Trust, who took him to Hickling Broad to see bitterns, harriers and bearded tits. Miss Gay, secretary of the Norwich and Norfolk Naturalist Society, showed him stone-curlews and crossbills in the Brecks.

He left Repton School for Cambridge with the firm intention of reading zoology, but was informed by his tutor on arrival at St John's that he would be studying economics instead. "I had always done what I was told to do," he remembered. And so a naturalist's career stalled before it had even begun. When

*John Henry Barrett, JB
to his friends.*

he barely scraped a pass at the end of the first year, he was persuaded to switch to geography.

On graduation, he set out with the intention of joining the Colonial Police in Burma, but a college secretary steered him onto a different path, suggesting that he take up a career tending the elephants that were used for logging teak forests in the vast jungles of Upper Burma. Malaria cut short his eastern adventure. A fever-ridden Barrett returned home and the same college secretary who had despatched him to Burma now advised him to join the RAF, offering the curious wisdom that a war was coming and those who were properly trained would stand a better chance of surviving it.

Barrett's active war career bordered on farce. Qualified as a pilot four days before the outbreak of war, he was sent to Shropshire to train bomb crews, though he had no personal experience of operations. It took two years before Barrett was finally sent for battle action. Not that he was in any hurry to go. He had married farmer's daughter Ruth Byass in 1940 and now had a baby daughter and another child on the way.

Name: **George Waterston**
Rank: **Second Lieutenant, Royal Artillery**
Date and place of birth: **10th April 1911, Edinburgh**
Education: **Edinburgh Academy**

With a cut-glass voice out of *The Prime of Miss Jean Brodie*, George Waterston was born into the crème de la crème of Edinburgh society. George Waterston & Sons Ltd, Edinburgh, printers and stationers, was founded in 1752 as makers of sealing wax. The family company was so much a part of the establishment that it was given the prestigious job of printing the Scottish pound note. Waterston went straight from Edinburgh Academy into "the Firm", as five generations of Waterstons had gone before him. But for the war, he might have spent the rest of his working life there.

A spare, lean man, Waterston had an underlying vulnerability. Throughout his life, he would be plagued with malfunctioning kidneys, a condition that would eventually kill him. Yet outwardly, nobody would have realised anything was amiss, for he possessed an extraordinary dynamic vitality. A former colleague remembered that "nothing would stand in his way if he wanted something done". Although an enthusiastic rugby player, most of his pre-war energy outside the workplace seemed to be devoted to birds. As a young teenager, he had learned his skills on family holidays and outings to the moors, taking eggs and keeping them in moss-lined drawers at home. He set up, together with a few family and friends, a group that he would transform, after leaving school, into the Midlothian Ornithological Club.

The young Waterston was a habitual visitor to the Royal Scottish Museum, where he met the keeper of natural history, Surgeon Rear-Admiral John H Stenhouse. The elderly ornithologist spoke at length about Fair Isle, the most remote inhabited island in Britain bar St Kilda, halfway between Orkney and Shetland. Stenhouse had taken over migration studies on the island from an equally eminent ornithologist with a wonderful

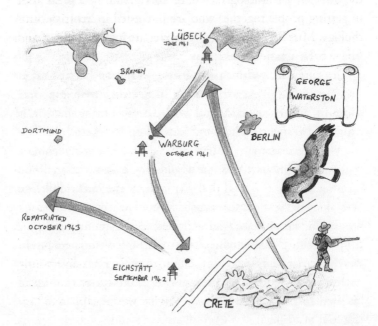

name – W Eagle Clarke. Stenhouse showed the impressionable boy the birds he had shot on the island, now stuffed and on display. The older man was looking for a successor. At the same time, two of Scotland's leading figures in ornithology, Evelyn Baxter and Leonora Rintoul, were keen to see the Isle of May in the Firth of Forth established as Scotland's first centre for migratory studies. The so-called "Good Ladies" won the day; Waterston tackled the challenge close to home first and was heavily involved in setting up and running the Isle of May as a cooperatively run bird observatory.

Two years later, in 1936, Waterston's drive had helped to see another project come to fruition: "We have now founded the Scottish Ornithologists' Club. This should be a great asset in getting people together who are interested in Scottish ornithology. Miss Rintoul and Miss Baxter are joint Presidents and I have been appointed secretary."

The following summer, Waterston set out on his first expedition abroad. It proved to be a hair-raising adventure. He travelled to Finnish Lapland with fellow birdwatcher JHB Munro and unwittingly found himself on the Russian side of the ill-defined border. Waterston was arrested and taken to a border cell, where he was interrogated by a Soviet officer who sat with a revolver on his desk throughout the interviews. The Scot spent several days in captivity, but the experience wasn't wasted. When he wasn't being grilled, Waterston occupied his time watching the activities of a pair of red-throated pipits, which were nesting next to the border post. The naïve young birdwatcher would regale others with the story for the rest of his life. It was a strange foretaste of what would happen to him just four years later.

In the years leading up to the outbreak of war, much of Waterston's considerable energy was channelled into the place that would come to dominate his life. He first went with a friend to Fair Isle in 1935. They were the only visitors that year and the first birdwatchers to land on the island in five years. The trip had an inauspicious beginning: "The boat was pitching and tossing and spray lashing over the bows… the sight of the lamp swinging about was too much… I retired to my bed." Once on dry land, he met the island's two resident ornithologists, Jerome Wilson and George "Fieldy" Stout, while his companion shot and skinned a red-backed shrike. That night, Waterston slept in the same bed an illustrious predecessor had occupied half a century before. The birdwatching Duchess of Bedford dubbed her accommodation Ortolan Cottage after her sighting of a rare ortolan bunting that day. The locals always knew it as the Pund.

Waterston returned to Fair Isle every summer until war broke out. He was befriended by George "Fieldy" Stout and stayed with him on his long holidays there. Fair Isle was a tough place:

Once I arrived to find Fieldy gutting a sheep on the kitchen table. We lived on that sheep for a fortnight but when I saw Fieldy about to throw the head on the midden I suggested that he should make sheep's heid broth. That evening I lifted the lid of a great black pot boiling on the fire to see what was for dinner, and there was an appalling greasy scum with the sheep's heid boiling merrily in the middle, complete with eyes, teeth and wool!

In his early years, Waterston followed an old-school approach to ornithology. Everywhere he went, he carried a pair of binoculars and a gun; the former to spot birds, the latter to shoot them. In those pre-ringing days, both Stenhouse and Stout still held to the accepted view that the only way to properly identify a bird was to shoot a specimen. But Waterston, encouraged by a visit to the Isle of May from Ronald Lockley, creator of Britain's first bird observatory, was soon keen to pursue the methods being instigated by Lockley and his contemporaries of catching

A gun and binoculars man. George Waterston pictured on Fair Isle in 1936.

and ringing instead of killing. However, his attempts to secure support and funding from the newly established British Trust for Ornithology towards renovating a cottage on the island came to nothing. War was coming and it was clear Waterston's ambition to set up a bird observatory on the island would just have to wait.

Supporting POW roles played by:

AJB "Barney" Thompson, Richard Purchon, George Raeburn, Maurice Waterhouse, Ernest Edlmann, Vincent Hollom, Captain The Earl of Hopetoun, Bertie Evers, ANL "Tim" Munby, Ian Pitman, Dick Winn, Tim Dooley, John Cripps, Dorrien Belson.

"I'm not a soldier"

On the day the Second World War broke out, Cheshire naturalist AW Boyd had one eye on the country diary column he was writing for the *Manchester Guardian*: the other he had lost on the battlefields of Gallipoli in 1915. An old soldier knew better than anyone about the realities of war. That day, he penned words for the paper which, had they gone wider, would have spoken to nature lovers everywhere, irrespective of nationality:

> I cannot help thinking that if only Hitler had been an ornithologist, he would have put off the war until the autumn bird migration was over. I wonder if any of the friendly Germans whom we met last year at the International Ornithological Congress at Rouen feel as I do. That he should force us to waste the last week of August and the first fortnight of September in a uniform that we hoped we had discarded for good is really the final outrage.

For the first eight months of "action", both sides relived the Great War on the Western Front, except that nothing much happened and hardly anyone got killed. British soldiers took to northern France the same weapons that their fathers and uncles had carried before them, and dug trenches in the clay just as their predecessors had done. By day, the sentries on the Maginot Line looked through their field glasses at German infantrymen, who really did hang out their washing on the Siegfried Line. By night, the Germans communicated with each other by hooting like owls. And everyone waited. Young men, primed for battle, relieved their tedium in the local bars and brothels. The impasse drifted on into the spring. Back in Britain, people began calling it the Phoney War. On 7th May 1940, a fed-up Peter Conder was granted home leave.

Three days later, the German blitzkrieg began, a massive air assault backed by tanks and troop carriers that tore through neutral Holland and Belgium. For the Allied forces, resistance quickly became a retreat, and then turned into an inglorious rout. Within a fortnight, Belgium had capitulated, fleeing troops had reached the beaches of Dunkirk and an evacuation began that saw a third of a million soldiers plucked to safety.

Winston Churchill's crucial morale-boosting "we shall fight on the beaches... we shall never surrender" address to the House of Commons and the listening free world on 4th June 1940, just 23 days into his premiership, was a masterpiece of oratory, but it was also cleverly and cruelly selective with the truth. "We got the army away," declared Churchill. But that wasn't quite the whole story. The Allied army had been split in two and more than 50,000 men were driven south by German divisions under the command of General Erwin Rommel. They were still fighting as Churchill spoke.

The junior officer who had been given home leave just before battle commenced did not rejoin his unit. At just 21 years old, Conder had already shown his eagerness by answering a call for trained officers to come forward, and had joined up with the 51st Highland Division. His erstwhile colleagues in the Signals Corps made it to the coast. Conder was later told that they boarded the passenger liner SS *Lancastria*, only for a German bomber to sink their ship, sending the soldiers and thousands of civilians to their deaths. Meanwhile, Conder was impatient for a piece of the action, On 1st June, he wrote to his father: "I am just about as 'browned off' as I could be. Practically nothing doing, except waiting to be posted. Actually I suppose I am in a better position than most, for I am 'standing by' that means I may go at any time."

Three days later, on the very day of Churchill's great speech, Conder sent his father a second and final letter as a free man, from the British Expeditionary Force base camp in Normandy: "Bit by bit I am progressing and very shortly I shall be with a unit. We arrived here in the early hours of yesterday morning and had to march eight miles in the dark. It was my first experience of night marching and I liked it. It was very cool compared with the colossal heat of the day... I expect that once I get to my unit, I shall be able to receive letters. At the moment, I haven't stayed in any one place to receive news."

Peter Conder's active service in battle lasted just seven days. But in that one week, he was thrown into fighting of terrifying intensity. Twenty years later, his young son David would ask the naïve question that all boys of that generation must have asked their soldiering fathers: "Daddy, did you ever kill anyone?" The boy remembered his father becoming very angry, saying: "It was very frightening, there were lots of bullets flying around. You could see the German soldiers, that people around you were being killed." Many years later, a war psychologist concluded that three-quarters of all combatants deliberately aimed over the heads of the men before them: was Peter Conder one of the compassionate majority who shot to miss and could not possibly admit to it?

Conder was part of a substantial force that was divided from the main army and pushed south into Normandy. They held the Germans briefly at the River Somme, then withdrew in the face of superior numbers and weaponry until they were surrounded in the tiny harbour port of St-Valery-en-Caux, a pretty little pre-war Balamory that was quickly pounded into ruins by German artillery firing from the hill above. The accompanying French troops of the 2nd Army, a motley collection of volunteers, lacked the stomach for a fight. At a point when the Highland Division had the German army in their sights, a ragged column of French soldiers walked into the line of fire, waving white flags of surrender. The British commanding officer, the unfortunately named Major-General Fortune, ordered his troops to shoot all French deserters.

It soon became apparent, as supplies of ammunition began to run out in the town, that defeat was inevitable. Out at sea, beyond the harbour, the slightly famous son of an extremely famous father was part of a Royal Navy attempt to evacuate the besieged troops. Lieutenant Peter Scott, an Olympic bronze medal winner in the 1936 Berlin Olympics, and son of the Polar explorer and national hero Captain Scott, was embarkation officer on board HMS *Broke*. He succeeded in guiding his ship into the harbour, but managed just one landing at St-Valery.

In less than an hour the ship was able to take on board only 125 men, before the shelling from above made it impossible to linger. A quarter of a century later, Scott and Conder would meet often as giants of the conservation movement. But there were to be no introductions here.

There were precious few opportunities for the navy to effect rescue operations inside a narrow harbour that was subjected to intense bombardment: most soldiers were unaware that they had even tried. The men looked out over the sea to the ships on the horizon and saw nothing happening. Many were so desperate to escape that they tried to climb down the cliffs surrounding the town, only to fall to their deaths on the rocks below. The rest were under the impression that they had been abandoned by their own side.

The German army pushed into the town itself and the two sides fought in unevenly matched hand-to-hand combat. When their ammunition had gone, Major-General Fortune ordered his troops to surrender, but Conder was among a group of thirteen soldiers who were unaware of the command. They simply went to ground, hiding in a cellar, hoping to sit things out before making a break for one of the other Channel ports. But the next day, their refuge was found and Conder heard a German officer say the words that would be uttered to hundreds of thousands of trapped soldiers over the coming years: "For you, the war is over."

Capture did not bring an end to the soldiers' ordeal. Exhausted through lack of sleep and food, and bewildered by the rapid course of events, the men were drilled by equally exhausted German troops into a marching column. Suddenly relieved of fighting duties, the British soldiers were dangerously punch-drunk. Peter Conder recalled a collective cocky sense of disbelief at their situation. The edgy captors issued an order that any step out of line to the left or right would mean instant death. One young man dared to break rank and was promptly shot dead. Every one of the soldiers was made to walk past his body.

For the next two weeks, the officers, by now divided from their men, were forced to march through the detritus of war, the ground littered with soldiers who died with their tin hats

Still kicking: the note Conder sent to his father to say he was alive.
It was attached to the covering letter from the Red Cross (left).

on. Every day, a dawn "meal" of coffee (that is to say, ground acorns) was all that would sustain their empty stomachs until they halted for the night. They walked twelve, fifteen, sixteen miles a day in blazing sun or pouring rain, not knowing where they were going, sometimes sleeping out in the open, so cold that they took the greatcoats off the bodies of men who had been killed only days before. The marching column – two or three thousand strong – was goaded to walk faster. There was no mercy for those who lagged at the back. One was bayoneted to death; the crack of a pistol told the men another comrade had been shot out of sight. Weary soldiers urged their weaker comrades on. French civilians put down pails of milk or threw the soldiers food as they passed – at some risk to themselves. Sometimes, the guards kicked the milk over. At other times, the men were able to snatch the chance to buy cherries, butter or chocolate when they stopped for the night in a village. It was a welcome addition to the ladle of watery soup that would otherwise be their only sustenance.

As they passed through the town of Lille, girls of the Red Cross rushed up to the officers and demanded their addresses: "We will write to your parents and tell them you are alive," they said. Peter Conder found a scrap of paper and scribbled the words that his family would receive after an agonisingly long three-month silence: "Taken prisoner. Still kicking."

Two hundred miles and a fortnight after they set off, the soldiers reached the Rhine and boarded a steamer. One fellow marcher wrote: "Two thousand officers of all nationalities huddled together on her decks and in her holds. If you turned over you hit your neighbour in the face. This was reality, field grey uniform, overcrowding, stink and hunger."

Worse was yet to come. At Nuremberg station, the men were crammed into cattle trucks, eighty in each, and endured two and a half days in a windowless wooden box with little food or sleep. On 7th July, wearing the same clothes that they had been captured in nearly a month before, the train arrived at their final destination, the POW camp of Laufen, a castle on the Austrian border. They could not know that five full years of captivity lay ahead of them. For Peter Conder, a life with meaning was about to begin.

* * *

It seemed appropriate that George Waterston, who carried both binoculars and a gun, should volunteer as a Territorial with the Royal Artillery. He was called up as soon as war began and, like Peter Conder, missed the first piece of the action – he was on leave in Edinburgh when the first Luftwaffe attack of the war struck the naval dockyard at Rosyth in October 1939. Waterston spent the whole of 1940 on the islands of the Firth of Forth that were fortified with gun emplacements to guard the estuary from the threat of invasion. He kept bird records, of course. A little auk was washed up on Cramond Island in January and on 1st May, he reported: "Whimbrel 1 shot (and eaten!)."

The year 1941 began with Waterston's unit boarding a troopship bound for Crete. They were among reinforcements sent into the Mediterranean to strengthen Greece in its fight against Italy. A nineteen-year-old midshipman who later became Prince Phillip, the Queen's consort, was on board one of the ships guiding the troops to the island. The men of the

207 Coast Battery took up a position just to the east of Chania. Lieutenant George Waterston did what he always did. The Mediterranean was a new country and there were new birds to see: "Sardinian warbler First seen 20/4/41. Like a small black-bird but with prominent red eye rims. Noted that on alighting, the tail feathers were spaced out." Waterston wrote SECRET on the cover of his birding notebook. It would not do for such information to fall into enemy hands. Years later, after he had brought the book home, he lent it out, saying: "Afraid my notes are very scrappy; largely compiled while dodging about in fox holes etc."

The last birding entry was written on 10th May. "Woodchat shrike One seen in Olive groves." Much later, in a POW camp, Waterston would write: "Little bird watching was accomplished during May due to the exigencies of war service; this was unfortunate as many summer visitors and passage migrants were on the move during that time." By the spring, Germany had shored up the faltering Italian troops, and ten days after Waterston's woodchat shrike, the Luftwaffe had begun an aerial bombardment of the Allied soldiers. Five days later, the German invasion of Crete began. Thousands of paratroopers rained down from the sky onto Maleme airfield, just ten miles from where Waterston's unit was based. Seven hundred and fifty more came by glider to the north side of the bay. All of the German troops were far better equipped than the Allied soldiers. More invaders poured in by air and sea and very soon, the Allied positions were overrun. Waterston knew it was time to take precautionary action, so he buried the pair of binoculars given to him by a Dundee professor years before.

Waterston's birds of Crete notebook. It bears an Oflag XC stamp, showing that the contents were read and approved at the Offizierlager Lübeck, where he arrived in the summer of 1941.

He and his men were now out of ammunition, so they made for the coast and a ship that was evacuating Allied troops. But there was not room for all of the soldiers, so they drew lots. Waterston was among those who lost. He found a British soldier disguised as a Cretan shepherd, tending a herd of goats. Waterston thought this was a good wheeze and tried negotiating with another goatherd for his animals. "Go and get your own goats" was the gist of the reply in whatever language it was expressed. Now, in Waterston's words, "It was like cowboys and Indians", as the men took to the hills in a bid to evade the invading force.

In the baking hot sun of a Cretan spring, the fleeing soldiers' food ran out and their only source of water came from draining the radiators of wrecked vehicles. Under terrible conditions of hunger and extreme thirst, Waterston's already vulnerable health deteriorated rapidly. By the time the men were captured on 1st June, he was gravely ill with cholera, dysentery and the beginning of stomach ulcers. The soldiers were shipped to Salonika, then put on trains bound for Germany.

As Waterston lay prone on the floor of a cattle truck, he overheard an Australian soldier betting a packet of fags that the critically ill Scot would be dead by morning. Barely conscious, Waterston resolved that he would not only last the night, he would bloody well survive the war.

* * *

Just twelve months after they were married, John and Marjorie Buxton were parted. His knowledge of Norwegian had made him perfectly qualified for signing up with the 1st Independent Company (later 1st Commandos), who were to be sent on a mission just inside the Arctic Circle. Buxton went reluctantly, and not just because he was parting from his new bride. Early in 1940, he had written to his old tutor:

I hope you'll find time to write me a letter or two while I'm being a soldier. I'm not a soldier and I want to hold hard to as much of the real life – New College, Norway, poetry, birds, wandering about hills and forests on ski, on foot and the sea – as I can. The other is only a sort of nightmarish interlude. I may wake up or I may not, that doesn't worry me. The thing is that someone should wake up.

Buxton boarded a ship heading far to the north. Hitler had sent an invading army into Norway in early April 1940 to secure supply routes for Swedish iron ore. Norway had capitulated, but there were still pockets of resistance. The Allies had already sent a force to capture the northern port of Narvik – a major outlet for the essential metal. Buxton's unit was under orders to block German relief troops heading north. They were equipped with skis, a month's rations of pemmican (dried meat and fat), small arms and no training in the guerrilla warfare for which they were sent. Seventy or so men sailed into a fjord to the calls of lamenting kitti-wakes and piping oystercatchers, sounds that Buxton had heard on Skokholm only the previous summer. He saw an early migrant – a swallow, dark-winged against the winter snow – and promptly dashed off a letter to Ronald Lockley in Pembrokeshire. The Skokholm warden later told the story of the moment he heard Buxton was reported missing in action: as he sat despondent at his desk, a swallow flew in through the open window and landed in his hand. Lockley was convinced this was a sign his brother-in-law was safe. And being a prac-tical man, Lockley ringed the exhausted bird and sent it on its way a few recuperative hours later.

On 10th May, the day France was overrun, German troops landed in the fjord close to the British commando unit. Buxton's platoon, travelling overland on skis, were dive-bombed by Stukas, and fought a brief battle in the streets of Mo i Rana with the Germans. It would be nearly two and a half years before he could bring himself to write down in verse what he had done that day:

The joy of battle – that I never knew
(The more's my loss) unless the joy should lie
In the curled, waiting finger, and watchful eye
Sifting each distant movement through and through.
But when that crawling shape came into view
Over the steady sights, what joy had I
To see it jerk, fling out an arm, and die?"

from Sonnet 5, written 19th August 1942

That evening, Buxton was one of half a dozen soldiers surrounded in a wooden farmhouse and taken prisoner. Their captors lined them up against the wall to shoot them… and then changed their minds.

* * *

After two years of training other pilots to fly into battle, one airman's turn finally came. Squadron Leader Barrett was posted to RAF Linton, near York, and on 15th September 1941, he left his wife and family and set off to command his first mission, stepping into the Halifax bomber, a type of aircraft that he had flown for the first time only the day before. The air raid target that night was Hamburg, but they never got that far. Caught in searchlights, the plane was brought down by ground fire before it had even dropped its load. Barrett baled out, not over Hamburg, as the navigator had led the crew to believe, but near the Baltic city of Kiel. Barrett parachuted down into a field: "Now a new urgency put speed into releasing all my trappings – quick, quick – it was half done, enough to allow me to have a pee. Never did a man derive a greater boost to morale than I did from that pee in the middle of the night alone in a ploughed field in Schleswig-Holstein." Barrett set about hiding his parachute, then, exhausted, went to sleep in a haystack. He awoke the next morning to find a farmer and two labourers standing over him. Squadron Leader Barrett's first mission was also his last.

Migration South

Reprieved from execution in front of a makeshift firing squad in northern Norway, John Buxton and his fellow commandos were transported by seaplane to Trondheim in the middle of the country, then billeted at a nearby aerodrome. They were among the first British prisoners of the Second World War. When he heard a chiffchaff singing outside, Buxton was inspired to compose two verses of poetry:

The Prisoner to the Singing Bird

Sing on, sing on beyond the walls
That I within may know
Spring is in the woods again
Where you may go

Sing on, sing on; then in my cage
I shall delight to hear
That you are glad and free out there
So near, so near!

The men were set to work loading supplies and repairing the aerodrome, but they were in grave danger from repeated bombing by RAF planes. Buxton walked around their compound, surreptitiously marking out a Union Jack with his feet in the dirt. On the next raid, one of the planes gave a victory roll of recognition and the attacks ceased.

Under orders to fuel the Luftwaffe planes and repair the runways, the prisoners managed acts of sabotage, watering down petrol or putting sugar in the fuel tanks.

From the compound, Buxton could see the tops of birch trees and faraway snow-capped mountains:

> The sky was my main view, and there I watched the birds flying over on migration northwards: whimbrel and redshank, geese, merganser and other duck, swallows and martins. I also watched the German aircraft go out and counted them; when they came back I counted them again. Sometimes they would crash in a pother of black smoke on the neighbouring hills, probably as a result of our attention to the fuel: it was difficult, but wise, to refrain from cheering. Sometimes they overturned on landing and then, as after each raid by our own machines we would watch the Germans making crosses of birch-wood.

At the beginning of June, Buxton was one of four soldiers sent south towards Oslo. As their train slowed through the bogs of Fokstumyra, where Buxton had seen his first nesting cranes two years before, he attempted an escape from a toilet window, but the gap was too narrow. In the city of Oslo itself, he led his captors on a great diversionary walk, hoping that a familiar face would come to rescue him, but no friendly Norwegian was forthcoming. The men were shipped to Denmark, and then transported by train to Hamburg. At each change of guard, the prisoners claimed they had not been fed yet. They managed seven meals in one belt-straining day. Their relatively comfortable progress continued – they even rode with their ubiquitous armed escort on Berlin's underground railway – until they reached the POW camp at Thorn, a fort on the Polish–Russian border:

> It was crowded with British troops from the West, many exhausted and dying after their march across Europe into captivity, sick with dysentery or pneumonia, brown and thin and worn… The camp was filthy and stank, and even if you lay in the sun on the grass-covered ramparts you were likely to rise up with lice in clothes and hair. Fleas we soon came to disregard as merely a nuisance; lice we were more afraid of. At one place in the grass a German notice warned us not to trample on a bird's nest – it was a tree pipit's – pleasing evidence of someone's concern with wild creatures to whom our savage antics were incomprehensible.

Buxton's stay was mercifully short; less than a week later, he and his companions were loaded into a French cattle truck with HOMMES 40 BETES 8 (room for 40 men or 8 cattle) stamped on its side. They were transported south to Laufen, where John Buxton would share his captivity with Peter Conder, though, astonishingly, the two men never met there.

"In the bag"

Oflag VIIC/H
8 July 1940

Dear family, I hope that by now you will have heard I am still alive. I have got to my final destination and everything is much better. The view from our window is magnificent. I hope to hear from you soon. You may write as often as you like at the moment. Cigarettes and chocolate are needed urgently also concentrated food in parcels.

    Love Peter

On his first full day in camp, 21-year-old Peter Conder wrote the upbeat "weather is lovely wish you were here" postcard that he hoped would give his family back home some reassurance. He might have wanted to add that he was in the snow-capped Bavarian Alps, staying in a castle on the Austrian border that had once been residence to the Archbishop of Salzburg, and that from his bedroom he had a view over the mountains to the spires in the city of Mozart's birth. He omitted to mention that those idyllic mountains lay beyond twelve-foot double perimeter fences of barbed wire, separated by coils and coils of more barbed wire, a barrier that was watched round the clock by guards in sentry towers carrying loaded machine guns. Or that the day before he had crawled out of a cattle truck after 60 hours' containment, his head shaved as an act of ritual humiliation, and that he was now sharing a room the size of the family lounge with three-tiered bunks and eighteen other men providing him with a nightly lullaby of farts, snores and restless dreams.

And what did time mean? – Conder had had his watch stolen by his captors, a bunch of trigger-happy Great War veterans, who showed the contempt that only victorious soldiers can show to vanquished foes. At night, they fired into the open windows of rooms whose blackout blinds were not drawn properly and

then shot at the men who tried to close them. And when the prisoners' own lights had gone out, searchlight beams swept round the boundaries and through the camp all night long.

This was the reality of Laufen Offizierlager VIIC (Laufen officers' camp, always abbreviated to Oflag. The Roman numerals refer to the district; in this case Bavaria). But none of the true detail of his situation would ever reach home – for the next few years, Conder's every written thought would be scrutinised and censored so that nothing critical would reach England. In a sense, confined with exclusively male company and forever under the control of others, he was back at public school, except that here the masters could shoot you.

Laufen Castle: from The Quill, *a POW camp magazine which began publication in March 1941.*

For the rest of the summer and into autumn, Conder received no letters or news from home and, in a grossly overcrowded camp of some 2,000 men living on near-starvation rations, his physical condition deteriorated. Another soldier remembered him "getting thinner and thinner".

Fellow lieutenant John Buxton, then unknown to Conder, noted: "We soon became so feeble through the lack of food that if we walked upstairs to our room we had a 'black-out' and had to lie down for a few minutes… Our ribs and joints stuck out more and more and our bellies swelled with the diet of stinking potatoes and cabbage soup." A group of American civilians came on an official visit to the camp as neutral observers, looked into Buxton's room and remarked: "You poor bastards."

The survivors of the battle at St-Valery had suffered more psychological damage than many of their fellow prisoners. Depressed by feelings of abandonment by their own side and starved of contact with their loved ones, they were fed a diet of German newspapers and camp loudspeakers telling stories of relentless victory. Plagued by dysentery (at any one time, one in ten of the prisoners was affected as a result of the diet), their all too regular visits to the toilet block were interrupted by guards offering persistent jibes: "*England kaput*" or "London in six weeks". The insinuations came to be known as latrinograms. One room-mate of Peter Conder voiced his pent-up frustration by repeating endlessly "bugger, bugger, bugger" as he lay in his bunk. A captain spoke of the men "lying in a state of listless apathy" on the beds where they ate, lived and slept. They talked about when the war might end. Many officers thought it would be over within a year. Conder felt two years was more likely. When the respected dean of a Cambridge college voiced his carefully assessed opinion that the war couldn't possibly end within two years, he caused acute depression all round. Most men kept their darkest thoughts to themselves, including the ever-present possibility that they could be killed by their captors at any time.

Despite the veneer of officer civility, primal instincts were never quite held in check. Near starvation gave rise to an attitude common to people living under such conditions. One prisoner wrote: "Personally I feel now that I would not trust a soul in this place and I am sure that almost any officer would do his brother down, not so much by stealing... but by wangling (so long as he is not observed) so that his share was the largest or at any rate not the smallest."

Gradually, the prisoners came to understand the necessity for outward camaraderie that would enable them to regain self-respect and build some kind of group solidarity. A slang language developed: their captors (and all Germans for that matter) were nicknamed "Goons" after troll-like cartoon characters popularised in the *Daily Mirror*. The German appellation of *Kriegsgefangenen* (prisoners of war) became shortened, so that the men blithely passed themselves off as "Kriegies". They were not in prison, but what they called "in the bag". And they talked endlessly about food and the future. At first they spoke of favourite pubs and restaurants and idealised menus. And then, when the past was too distant and too painful to remember, they planned for the magical time "after the war" when they would build better lives at home.

Conder's own inner state of mind during those first few months can be gauged by that most reliable barometer – his birdwatching. More than 50 years later, he said that during that time he didn't do any birdwatching at all, his passion drained by physical and mental exhaustion: "It shook me rigid being put in the bag," he once confessed in a rare moment of soul-baring.

* * *

On 1st October 1940, Conder received his first letters from England and their arrival seemed to lift his spirits. He celebrated by writing back to his family using the wry British sense of humour that would more than once evade the censor's obliterating pencil: "After parade in the morning we wait for lunch which usually consists of airpie and then for tea, which is quite often windy pudding. With these two substantial meals we pass the day quite happily." Two weeks later, he commented:

> The Red Cross seem to have a strange idea of what we can do here and [are] telling people to send golf clubs, tennis rackets and white flannels. We laugh. Our exercise ground is about twice as large as our garden and when everyone is out it is rather worse than Hampstead Heath. But you usually manage to find a time, when there are not too many people out, to walk round and round, rather like white mice, for an hour or so.

Seven years older than Conder, and an organiser by inclination, John Buxton had realised from the very beginning of his captivity that the prisoners' greatest immediate enemy was boredom, a listless nothingness that allowed doubt and fear to prey on their minds. He wrote to Marjorie at the end of his second week: "If I could get some work to do on birds – since there's not much hope of continuing my work on RB* here – then the time would pass much more quickly, and wouldn't be wasted. That's the worst thing – wasting time."

In Laufen, as elsewhere, the officers were free from work duties. Menial tasks were carried out by a smattering of men from lower ranks, known by their officers as orderlies, who were given the castle stables as accommodation. The idle elite needed to devise other ways to occupy their time. Effortlessly accomplished in the arts, Buxton set up an English literature club three days after he arrived at Laufen, with himself elected as president:

> For the duration of one war: this used to meet each Sunday to read papers written by the members, or extracts selected from any books they might find. We even had "dinners" to which each member brought his slice of bread and piece of potato, which it became conventional to decorate in some manner, perhaps by shaping the potato when mashed into the form of an animal or by inserting in its bleak surface some ornament made of bread or cheese. At these dinners each member had to read some topical, and usually scurrilous or seditious, verse of his own composition.

Buxton's "dinners" formed part of a series of lectures and discussions promoted within what the prisoners called the

---

* Buxton had begun (and never completed) a doctorate on the former Poet Laureate Robert Bridges.

"University of Laufen – the only university which rigorously excludes women and is much easier to enter than to leave".

Buxton was enduring the agony of a man completely cut off from his wife: "Still not a word from you or of you in almost 6 months' absence. The largest mail yet from England came in yesterday but so far nothing for me… it is very distressing not to know how and where you are." He paced the exercise ground and walked down to a patch of land known as "the garden", overlooking the left bank of the River Salzach, where he watched for birds. Towards the end of his life, Peter Conder recalled a September day on which John Buxton was watching birds and he was watching Buxton:

> I saw him standing on the top of a bank and looking down into a small stream that ran into the River Salzach. He was quite obviously birdwatching. A year or two later after I had been sent to two camps in Poland I found out that his name was John Buxton and he told me that he had been watching black-necked grebes. It is a measure of my birdwatching abilities at the time that I did not recognise them.

One bird in particular drew John Buxton's attention, one noted for its delicate grace and beauty: "In the summer of 1940, lying in the sun near a Bavarian river, I saw a family of redstarts, unconcerned in the affairs of our skeletal multitude, going about their ways in cherry and chestnut trees."

By late autumn, Buxton had established contact with his wife, sending bird-tinted letters that tried to comfort her: "I am in lovely country, which won't surprise you after your dream but barbed wire cuts me off from the mountains, but there are green fields and trees near me. Of birds I've seen black-necked grebes, black redstarts, serins, icterine warblers etc."

He sent Marjorie a postcard with a poem that drew out his thoughts while watching a parade-ground tree:

"I did not recognise them" – black-necked grebes in winter plumage.

Lime-tree

You are too proud, my lime-tree
Standing in silence there
A pillar of green, curling smoke
In motionless air

We who walk round and round you
Like brown leaves blowing by
Remind you that in windy autumn
Your leaves will fly

Yet why should you care, my lime-tree
Though all your twigs are bare
And rustling leaves blow by your feet –
Why should you care?

At about that time, a letter arrived in camp that was to have profound consequences for both Buxton and those who would help him in future. It had been written and posted from Pembrokeshire by his brother-in-law Ronald Lockley, on the day Lockley had received a telegram from Marjorie saying that her husband had been captured alive. Perhaps some lines of this letter would have been erased by the censor by the time it reached Buxton months later, or it may have been embellished later by Lockley. However, the essence is clear:

> You will no doubt deeply regret the circumstances that
> have resulted in your imprisonment. But these were beyond
> your control, and must be accepted with the philosophy

*The cobbled yard at Laufen: in wet weather, the only place where
1,700 inmates could exercise.*

with which your mind, as I well know, is fully equipped.
To us the prospect of a long separation – for it will surely
take a year or so for unprepared Britain to recover from this
impact of the highly armed and prepared Nazi machine –
grim as it is, is offset by the thought that you are safe... in
your prison camp you will no doubt, as an officer, have some
if not much leisure in which to think and read and write.
You will in a sense be as enisled [trapped on an island] as
we are, and your observations will be limited to the fauna
of that entity of your camp and its perimeter. This should
give you the chance of concentrating particularly on one

or two species as I have done here, and making a study of great interest.

The contents of that letter would have to stay swirling in Buxton's brilliant mind for months to come. At that time he had neither paper nor reference books. And the Bavarian winter was beginning to bite. On 3rd November, London had its first night without an air raid since 7th September and the first flakes of snow fell on Laufen Castle. Temperatures dipped to eighteen degrees below zero. Conder wrote home:

The Yugo-Slaw Red Cross sends me two parcels a month, containing biscuits, bacon and cigarettes etc. Except for the bacon, it all goes the same day and for one evening my tummy is full at bed time. The British Legion may be sending me a parcel from Switzerland until food parcels arrive from England. It is pretty chilly here these days. The snow is low on the mountains and the frost is thick on the grass and the sky looks very wintery. In fact a sharp walk would be a good order for the day. At night, the frost is very apt to creep down my spine, unless the blanket is tucked well round my neck.

Yet midwinter was far from bleak. Red Cross parcels from everywhere but Britain were now starting to trickle through. Private parcels from home were beginning to arrive too and the prisoners' efforts to provide themselves with spirit-raising entertainment were bearing fruit. Conder celebrated Christmas with the arrival of a sleeping bag and a seat at a prisoners' pantomime

POW artists produced works of exquisite subtlety to send covert messages to the outside world. The "holly" border on this Christmas card is typical.

performance of *McLaddin and His Wonderful Lighter*, featuring Welsh actor Desmond Llewellyn, who would later find a bigger stage as Q in the James Bond films. Buxton wrote to Marjorie on Christmas Eve: "I saw a Black Kite the other day: do you remember the one in Malaga? We have Xmas trees, streamers, tinsel."

By now, the prisoners were able to request and receive books from home. John Buxton took on the role of camp librarian. By the time he left the camp eighteen months later, he was keeper of more than 2,000 books. Conder's own requests to home were telling. He showed a token expression of interest in his profession by asking his father for a single book on advertising. However, appeals for Gilbert White's *Natural History of Selborne*, Cobbett's *Rural Rides*, *The Life of Audubon*, *Animal Behaviour*, *Flight of Birds*, WH Hudson's *Shepherd's Life* and Walton's *Compleat Angler* revealed where his true inclinations lay.

John Buxton made some sort of resolution at the beginning of 1941 to bring order, structure, purpose and control to his life: he decided to keep daily records of the birds he saw. This brought great comfort to Marjorie: "It sounds more like my John when you say you keep bird notes every day." Buxton kept records with meticulous detail, even to the point of knowing absurdity: "On July 13th and 14th a Canary was present in rooms 77 & 80 until ejected."

Conder was also looking outwards. At the end of the first week of January, he wrote home to say that he had spent some time looking into a backwater, the same stream where Buxton had looked the year before. In that same month, a prisoner painting the view from an upstairs window was ordered not to lean out of the window. When he failed to respond immediately, he was shot dead.

Within his own hut, Conder was quietly earning himself a reputation and a title. Messmate Ernest Edlmann recalled: "Oh yes, 'Birdie', that's what he was known as – a popular but silent chap with a marvellous infectious smile. Very interesting character and what he didn't know about birds wasn't worth knowing; he had an eye for them."

"So limited was the space that we had to sleep in three-tiered beds, the bottom one being one foot six inches off the floor, and the top one about six feet up. The occupant of the latter had to scramble like a monkey into his narrow and uncomfortable perch, and, if careless, was in constant danger of batting his head against the ceiling."
— TCF Prittie, Laufen inmate.

On 1st February 1941, the prisoners held an ice gymkhana on their frozen parade ground, with free skating, musical chairs and three-legged races the order of the day. The 5th of the month saw Buxton record in his elegant prose a crow attacking a kestrel: "Flight made in narrow spiral, crow continually attacking from below, kestrel eluding it by side slips and turns, after which it would sail for a few seconds. The birds appeared to separate when tiny specks and the kestrel flew off W before disappearing." By the end of February, the ice had melted and the parade ground turned into a quagmire. The thaw was cause for activity down by the river bank. A number of guards and orderlies began cutting down undergrowth on the land between the backwater and the river and extending the barbed wire perimeter, so that the prisoners could have an extra area in which to exercise. But Conder was not to enjoy the extended liberty. A fit of pique on Hitler's part was to send him elsewhere. News reached Berlin that German POWs in Canada had started a fire in their camp, rendering it uninhabitable. They were supposedly rehoused in a fortress that was below Geneva Convention standards. Hitler ordered a tit-for-tat. Conder knew nothing of this when he wrote to his uncle: "We are in a flap at the moment. A large number of junior officers, amongst them, myself, are going to Poland. Some people want to go, others do not mind. I am one of the latter." Rumours circulated that the camp where the men were to be posted would be a kind of Polish Sandhurst. Had he known better, he would have shown rather more concern.

It was doubly unfortunate for Conder that he left Laufen on the cusp of spring. In March 1941, John Buxton led the first ornithological initiative in the camp. He had sat through talks on heraldry, pig farming, beekeeping, income tax and the study of old handwriting in the dark days of the previous year, when each speaker's greatest achievement was to stay on his feet all the way through his talk, and each lecture was given to an apathetic "audience of comatose, shaven-headed sheep". Now Buxton felt the time and conditions were right to give half a dozen talks of his own. He spoke on a subject he knew intimately, the bird life of Skokholm. At the end of one lecture, a number of fellow prisoners came up to Buxton. They included Vincent Hollom, whose brother Phil was already making his mark in ornithology, and Richard "Dick" Purchon, a professional naturalist, though his chosen field of marine biology was perhaps not an advantage in a prison 150 miles from the sea. Yorkshireman Purchon was a brilliant scholar who followed up a first-class honours degree from Bristol University with a PhD completed at breakneck speed in just two years before war broke out.

The men resolved there and then to set up a birdwatching and naturalists' group. Buxton persuaded the now rather more obliging camp authorities that part of the newly acquired land known as "the island" should become a nature reserve. What was more, he arranged for the delivery of wood and the new naturalists' society built nine nestboxes and began putting them up. An enthused Dick Purchon wrote home: "Yesterday several swallows passed through on migration. If when the redstarts arrive some nest in one of my boxes, Buxton and I intend to watch their behaviour continuously (never done before) and perhaps write an article about it."

Buxton had already ruminated on Lockley's exhortation of the previous summer and settled on the common redstart as a bird for intensive observation. Although he had no reference books, he had a notion that this was a little-studied bird. There were practical reasons for its selection: watching a pair feeding their young within the grounds in 1940, he had observed that these conspicuous birds – the males and females easily distinguishable – were as tame as robins back home. Tolerance to disturbance would be an important factor in a place crowded with hundreds of men. Like their robin cousins, redstarts held small territories, so that their behaviour could be studied virtually all of the time. After all, an incarcerated ornithologist could not follow a bird that went beyond the wire. And the period of study could be neatly fixed between the arrival and departure dates of this migrant.

But Buxton also chose the redstart for a simple aesthetic reason: "It was more likely to be a pleasure watching so bright and gaily coloured a bird for the many hours that we intended to watch, than it would have been if we had chosen a dowdy and songless species."

In those first days of April, the naturalists sat outside and waited for the migrant birds to return from Africa. They saw a treecreeper "gathering fluff out of crevices in willow bark. This was the first bird seen preparing to nest". The two observant watchers also saw a convoy of ambulances drive over the bridge across the River Salzach. The vehicles were bound for Yugoslavia or Greece. Both countries were being overrun by the German army.

On 10th April, the bird that, more than any other, would come to be associated with Buxton, arrived from its wintering grounds: "Snow was falling, as it had been for the past three days, when the first cock redstart came into the patch which we euphemistically called 'the lower garden' and perched on the high retaining wall of the Palace, our prison."

As Buxton watched the bird searching for insects on the snow-free sheltered wall, two more males and a female arrived, staying close together. One male fluttered down to the stream, pecking continuously for drowned insects, washed down in the melting snow.

For the next five days, Buxton maintained his watch, but on 16th April, there came an interruption of the kind that would punctuate and disrupt observation repeatedly for the duration of the war. Somebody tried to escape.

"I chose the redstart because of its grace and beauty, and for the sweet gentle charm of its song." – John Buxton.

There were never any heroic escapes into neutral territory from Laufen. Nobody succeeded in escaping from the camp to freedom, just as precious few did from anywhere else. Buxton himself joined the team of diggers, willingly or otherwise, but later commented ruefully: "If ever I got my nose past the wire this was only at ten feet below ground level." The result of an escape attempt was hardship for every prisoner in the camp. All the rooms were searched. Buxton recalled one particularly tense incident: "One fellow prisoner, discovered under a bed, was asked if there was a tunnel there. He confessed that there was. The sentry, hoping to catch the criminals at the moment of discovering the crime, demanded to know who made it. "Two mice" was the reply.

Searches did not simply consist of an interrogation and a rifling through possessions. Invariably, all of the prisoners' belongings and often even their beds were thrown outside. Buxton remembered that some guards took a particular delight in throwing one boot of a pair at one end of the camp and the other boot at the opposite. The men were then made to stand to attention in all weathers through roll-calls that would last for up to eight hours. On that particular day, Buxton simply recorded in his notebook, with necessary understatement, that the camp was searched by the Germans and so he was unable to take any notes.

Camp searches were not the only hindrances to study. The birds did not keep to German timetables – Buxton and the faithful Purchon were allowed only six hours a day for observation and, at times, the guards stopped them in their watch, suspecting they were planning an escape. They had no binoculars, nor did they ever see any of the three nests at Laufen, for to do so would have meant scaling a wall, climbing a tree or borrowing a ladder and, as Buxton noted wryly, "these things were not encouraged". He could draw maps showing the location of the nests, but if the maps were seen, they were often confiscated by guards who suspected that the cunning prisoner might be mapping potential escape routes out, instead of marking the birds' nests within.

The first redstarts to arrive were merely passing through on migration elsewhere: when a breeding pair finally turned up they began darting after each other in courtship chases with speed, grace and beauty. They were everything the camp was not. The enraptured birdwatcher declared that "one of the chief joys of watching them in prison was that they inhabited another world than I".

Through the entire breeding season, Buxton and Purchon sat out together in all weathers, day after day, one watching, the other scribbling brief notes on cigarette packets, toilet paper – anything they could lay their hands on. Buxton had learned thoroughness from his brother-in-law. Record everything. Leave out nothing. The sifting and selection could come later. And so their field notes went into mind-numbing detail:

29.4.41 Song. Establishment of territory.
10.10 Flew onto barn roof.
10.11 Flew back to wires.
10.14 Back to low tree of orchard near hut.
10.19 Back to tree from ground. More song.
10.20 Down to stick in allotment.
10.21 Singing on woodpile in allotment.
10.22 Across to 1st chestnut.
10.24 Singing in 3rd chestnut at very top.
10.25 Along to 5th chestnut.
10.27 Across to lime tree.

But Buxton could also write with graphic, filmic precision. The vitality of observation and annotation was captured in notes scribbled down as he watched: "Runs along, stops, flicks tail, runs along, stops, flicks tail, again, again, up to further willow, flicks tail, song, to ground. Scolding. Two males flying about just over my head. Now in tree with Great Tits (nesting in box). Both close together, but silence."

The two birdwatchers were not exactly watching their quarry in peace. Buxton's description of the redstart's territory gives a sense of the level of interruption: "Disturbance by man constant and continuous from say 8am to 8pm + in area by nest – SW of creek and N of sentry-box. In territory on island disturbance only from 10 to 11am, 2 to 4pm, 5 to 7pm, and not constantly owing to shutting of island."

Marjorie Buxton held an idyllic picture of her husband's endeavours in her mind's eye: "I wonder if you are in your wood today – I like to think of you there. On your island. Especially when this lovely weather is about – watching birds and writing and watching flowers. It's a great joy to know you have this wood."

By 28th May, Buxton and Purchon were watching a brooding female and they noted: "Song difficult to observe due to much screaming of swifts from 8.15 to 9.20am and also noise of men walking about in large numbers." On that same day, several hundred miles to the south, the defeated British army began walking in large numbers onto ships as they began their evacuation of Crete.

Richard Purchon's willingness to share in the redstart vigil was reciprocated by Buxton, who assisted the Yorkshireman in wider natural history studies. A summer flood brought fish fry into the camp and the men rescued them and kept them for some weeks in a soup bowl. The opportunity for close examination delighted the marine biologist, but Buxton was not so enamoured. He showed even less enthusiasm for Purchon's next project – a study of door snails: "We pasted tiny pieces of coloured paper on the shells of some clausilia to watch their lethargic meanderings about an ancient wall: however, this proved a little tedious, even for prisoners." Purchon did not necessarily concur with Buxton's opinion. After the war, he became a world authority on marine molluscs.

News came through in late June 1941 that a German invasion had brought Russia into the war. The German army advanced 185 miles towards Moscow in four days. Buxton and Purchon were trying to track movements of a different kind. The young redstarts were fledging from their three nests. Restrictions on their viewing times meant that the men were denied the opportunity to see the maiden flights of the chicks from the first nest. Buxton could only conclude that they had fledged on one of two possible dates. Sometimes, the pair could see chicks being fed by their parents within the camp; at other times they could not be followed. On 1st July, Buxton noted with regretful tenderness: "I picked up an injured chick which died very soon in my hand. It had probably flown into the barbed wire."

The methodical naturalist recognised the enforced limitations to his diligence: "As I do not know how many eggs were laid in any of the three nests, nor how many chicks hatched, nor how many flew, I have no information on the incidence of mortality. The only chick known to have died after leaving the nest met with a somewhat unnatural accident, since aprons of barbed wire are not an integral part of the redstart's environment."

In August, Buxton received a most welcome billet doux from his wife: "Nest built apparently by hen wholly. Incubation chiefly by hen but cock has been seen on eggs. Incubation period 14 days has been recorded on continent…" Marjorie Buxton was an ongoing source of information on redstarts that summer, corresponding with ornithologists throughout Britain (including Harry Witherby, who supplied the above information) and sending on what she had acquired to her husband, who was without the precious ornithological volumes. But perhaps she had a thankfully idealised view of her husband's situation: "I expect you have made the most of your observations of redstarts in your bird sanctuary."

At the end of that month, the hot summer weather broke. On 1st September: "River flooded higher than ever before – over N end of island by noon, up to hand-rail on footbridge 7pm and still rising." On the following day, Buxton saw his last redstarts of the season: "Two birds in winter plumage by creek… in April, the first arrivals in the area were in this same territory."

* * *

As the redstart's voice was lost, Buxton found his. Sitting on the bank from which he had watched the birds, he now had time on his hands and poetry in his head. He began a lengthy work that would eventually see publication as *Westward*. The title itself evoked a promise of freedom, both spiritual and physical, the author imagining himself sitting on the cliffs at Skokholm looking out at a view over the ocean without barriers, without boundaries, seemingly without end. It contains passages suffused with observation, memory and reflections on his own condition:

> *But I have waked to hear in the small rain*
> *The chiffchaff's song again,*
> *And the returning willow-wren's light laughter*
> *Among green-misty trees, and the refrain*
> *Of cuckoo far away the moment after.*

And I have lain long hours upon the grass
Watching small insects pass
Whose wings are coloured like the light that streams
Through eyelashes half-closed, flies winged with glass,
Practical ants, and beetles drowsed with dreams.

I have seen thistledown, and feathery seeds
Of spiky fireweeds
Afloat on autumn wind; pulled sticking burrs
Out of my Harris; learned where the squirrel feeds
From the chawed cones lying beneath the firs.

I have seen the ferny foliage of frost
On window-panes embossed,
The brittle casing on the fallen leaves,
And grizzled grass-blades, and the twigs white-mossed,
And ridgy icicles hung from the eaves.

Thus the four-season pageant passes on
And soon the year is gone.
We count so many months, weeks, days, and hours,
Number the rain-drops; measure light that shone
Out of the sun: — knowledge like this is ours.

Westward appeared in print during Buxton's captivity, as did a subsequent collection of poems, which included both natural history and vivid accounts of his battle experience, published under the title of *Such Liberty*. One of the most beautiful and tender poems was "Hymn", written in prison, a love poem to his absent wife, containing a first verse of pent-up yearning:

I watch the quick, un-English river, grey
With thick snow-water from the spiky hills;
I see the children swimming in the creek,
I hear them laugh and speak
But cannot catch a word of all they say.
Upstream the dusty green of willows fills
The middle distance, and, beyond, the spires
Of churches where once Mozart taught the choirs
To sing his melodies. Beyond again
The sudden mountains rise up and invite
My cramped legs back to liberty, – in vain,
For everywhere the barbed wire snags my sight
As each day it will do
Till Peace returns and I come back to you.

Buxton's poems came to be read by the British public, first of all in magazines and newspapers, including the *Observer* and *Sunday Times*, later in book form, while he was still a POW. How was such a thing possible?

The erudite scholar habitually quoted large passages of verse in his correspondence. His wife read letters that were, in content, half her husband, half Homer. Inevitably, the German censors got to know the characters and stories of the individual prisoners, whose lives they scanned. In Buxton's writing, they must have grown wearily accustomed to sifting through Shakespeare sonnets and gobbets of the *Iliad*, and so when *Westward* found its way to Marjorie for publication, stuffed with classical references, German eyes must surely have glazed over. His war poetry received the same cursory dismissal. Maybe Milton and the ancient Greeks helped his words slip under the wire.

Summer turned to autumn and Buxton was aware of a growing sense of staleness in the camp. The men had lived in too close proximity for well over a year; they knew what their messmates would say before they spoke, knew the little habits that were beginning to prove irksome. Yet they had become institutionalised too and feared change. There was some trepidation when they heard they were to be moved. Buxton kept his equilibrium to make one last record at Laufen. Under "Swallow" he noted: "There were several flying about by the station on the morning we left Oct. 13 (a wet day)."

RETRIBUTION

For Peter Conder and his fellow junior officers, who had been led out of Laufen in March 1941, there must have been a dreadful sense of familiarity about boarding a train bound for an unknown prison camp. Each man was pressed shoulder to shoulder against neighbours on all sides. They waited in sidings for hours at a time as other trains were given priority. On the second evening of cramped tedium, the train rattled slowly through:

> a part of a town which had no architectural merit – the sort of buildings that one would expect in the poorer quarters of towns on the continent that had been fought over many times in the last two or three centuries. What caught our attention were the women sitting seductively in the first floor windows apparently trying to attract the attention of half-a-dozen German soldiers in the street below. Whether they were flattered or not they were also inspected by 200 to 300 British Officers who were of course powerless to implement the results of their inspection.

The men were disgorged into the darkness and marched through the town of Posen, kicked and prodded by guards who wanted to impress on the watching Polish civilians exactly who was in charge. They arrived, four weary miles later, at a huge fortress, built in the nineteenth century to protect the new German state's border from the threat of Polish invasion. The prisoners were housed, six to each broad bed, in its dark, dank subterranean bowels. A single light bulb gave bare illumination to the airless room, its window all but blocked, its floor lined with straw, wet from a leaking pipe. The men had company in their cell: it was seething with lice, fleas and bedbugs. For three weeks in late winter, the prisoners shivered and scratched at their bitten bodies, seeing little daylight except for rare occasions when they were allowed onto the fortress roof. There they looked out on a railway line, where day after day, wagons brimming with tanks thundered past. They guessed (correctly) that an attack on Russia was in the offing. And then the prisoners were told they were moving once again, this time a much shorter distance to a ring of forts that surrounded the town of Thorn. This was the POW camp where Buxton had spent a week in transit the year before. Here, Conder's companions scrawled their bitterness on the prison walls:

VALERIE
THE 51ST HEROES
WE ARE THE LITTLE BOYS THE BEF* FORGOT

---

* British Expeditionary Force – the name given to the land army in Europe during the first year of the war.

… and a defiant ring of patriotism:

GOOD OLD CHURCHILL
GIVE THE GERMAN Bs HELL

At the entrance to some rooms, they wrote but one word:

SILENCE.

Peter Conder put a positive spin on his new situation when he wrote home on 14th April 1941 – the first letter he had sent since leaving Laufen:

> Once again, I have been moved to another camp very much like the last, only slightly better. The country is not so flat and there are more trees about. It is an ancient fort like the last but slightly larger, and we can almost read in our rooms without the light. There are one or two things which make a great difference. We no longer have to wash our own plates, our laundry is well cleaned outside, and we get showers with hot water once more. It was only a short journey here, but my suitcase disappeared at the end of it and has been no more seen.

It was not just the condition of the new camp that brought a marked improvement: Red Cross parcels were starting to come through as well. Eight had arrived in the previous eight months; now they were coming at the rate of one every fortnight and men in each room shared out most of the contents, with chocolate and cigarettes particularly popular.

Spirits were lifted further when the prisoners were allowed to walk about on the grass-covered ramparts surrounding the fort:

I think in my last letter I complained about the coldness and lateness of spring; now the weather is at the other extreme. A few days ago it snowed; the following day the sun was baking; the day after, the leaves were fully out and the birds were in full song: the day after that it was too hot to go out between ten am and four pm. That was spring!

"I enclose a photograph of our arrival at XXID. I am up near the front on the right (invisible) inspecting the gaping monster." Conder's letter home of 13th September 1941 describing the prisoners entering Posen POW camp.

Inexplicably, sitting out on the grass, surrounded by trees, a hundred miles from the sea and some distance from any wetland, Conder decided to make wading birds his main topic of study and sat outside for hours at a time reading TA Coward's seminal *Birds of the British Isles*. He was also watching and listening to the birds around him. One day, he heard a loud fluting call, a sound unlike any other he had ever heard, coming from the trees on the outer ramparts. Then at last, he saw it, his first ever golden oriole, vivid yellow, as bright as the spring sunshine.

Two closely related birds began to absorb him. They were nesting only yards apart in a brick-walled moat at the foot of the rampart. A pair of black redstarts had taken up a hole in the wall just a few feet from the ground; a common redstart nest was under a tuft of grass just below. Although the birds occasionally chased each other, Conder was fascinated that two species occupying very similar ecological niches should nest in such close proximity. From time to time, the black redstarts would fly up to the top of the fort. On 23rd April, he noted that although the German guards had cleared the trees on the top of the fort to give themselves a wider field of fire over the prisoners, the posts that they had set up in their place provided replacement perches for the black redstarts. But he never found out whether the two pairs' nesting attempts were successful. Events in faraway Canada dictated the prisoners' next move. The Allies moved the German POWs from their sub-standard accommodation at Fort Heures to a more salubrious location, and so the German authorities decided to reciprocate.

"I could look out for any birds in the neighbouring wooded areas. I scored my first Golden Oriole there" – Conder writing of his birdwatching at Thorn.

Black redstart – a close relative of the robin, with the same alert, upright stance.

Just 40 miles from the Swiss border, 40 miles from freedom, purpose-built Oflag VB at Biberach in Wurtemburg was next in the trio of Conder's short-term residences:

> Whether the heat here is really any greater than at our last place I don't know, but it so hot that I cannot go out after 11am... We have left large buildings and are now in barrack blocks. They have many advantages, they are clean and airy. Three more good things are drinking water, washing and sanitation. The high pressure showers are the best I have seen. Disadvantages are overcrowding, which they say will be relieved as soon as possible and the scenery which except for the mountains in the background resembles the plains as to the amount of trees. They say we can see Switzerland on a clear day.

A walk around this camp was "approximately 680 yards, occupying five and three quarter minutes". In this flat, featureless landscape, there were few birds for Conder to watch. Skylarks, however, were ever present in the arable fields beyond the wire, and he set about transcribing their song. In time, as the birds fluttered up towards the heavens and invisibility, he was confident he could identify each individual by sound alone.

Conder's letters home in that summer of 1941 reveal a young man shedding a little of his habitual reserve. In July, he wrote:

> We are doing pretty well ourselves, though feeling extraordinary lazy, nothing extraordinary for me. I sleep most of the afternoon, with no ill effects on my log like repose at night. The trio has just moved into a small room with 3

new boys; one an Australian, another an architect, who decorates [one] wall with rather attractive young ladies… on the other we have Norfolk birds, Norfolk marshes, a seascape, and the latest is again of the marshes with racing [cars], done on a blue background with pieces of coloured paper, very effective.

For the one and only time during the war, he reproached his family: "Don't waste paper telling me to keep my chin up."

September began with Conder writing in a jocular, self-dep-recatory manner: "I am growing fat, got the disease known as the 'Kastoffel belly'. Nice layers of fat for winter… You will probably be surprised to hear that I have become energetic again, and every morning I read six or seven pages of a German book." Tolerably comfortable in his routine, regularly fed and watered, and lacking any responsibility, Conder was settling into a pattern of what prison psychologists would recognise as almost childish behaviour. But at the beginning of October, his indulgent lifestyle came to an end. Higher authorities had hatched a plan to incarcerate as many British officers as possible together in one super-camp. Conder was on his travels again. The men were taken north, this time to the plains around the Westphalian town of Warburg. Their guards for the journey were more used to transporting Russian prisoners and had become accustomed to behaving with abrupt brutality. At the station, one British officer made a run for freedom, then froze and raised his hands in surrender at the shout of "*Halt*!" But a guard standing six yards away shot him dead anyway.

ALL TOGETHER

On the morning of 16th September 1941, Squadron Leader John Henry Barrett woke up to find himself looking down the barrel of a gun. The night before, he had parachuted down from his blazing bomber into a farmer's field. From a barn in Schleswig-Holstein, where the dozing officer was discovered by the farmer and two labourers and taken into custody, it was a short, but inevitable journey to Oflag XC at Lübeck. On the way, he passed through a perfunctory interrogation at the hands of a German officer. By the summer of 1941, RAF officers quizzed for military information had learned the drill on capture. They disclosed their name, rank and number and nothing else. The normally talkative Barrett kept quiet.

Arriving at Lübeck, Barrett was given accommodation that befitted a squadron leader's status, though he shared his double room with five other officers. He and his RAF companions discovered their prison rations were meagre too. They quickly adapted by improvising. A fellow officer despatched the *Kommandant*'s cat that had slinked in under the barbed wire. It became a cat stew, though nobody remembered afterwards whether it tasted fair or foul. Barrett noticed that the camp's

73

previous use as a farm field had left a growing legacy in the shape of some turnips. He slipped between a gap in the trip wire and the perimeter fence when the guard wasn't looking and passed the vegetables in scrum-half fashion to an eager officer standing behind. That night, a dozen men ate what was, under the circumstances, a feast of cold turnip.

George Waterston had arrived at Lübeck in June, but his was a presence confined largely to the camp hospital. He was long enough in the camp proper to get the measure of the *Kommandant* and refer to him in Great War language as "an absolute Hun of Huns", but George now had stomach ulcers which kept him in bed. German doctors would eventually stitch up half of his stomach.

In mid-October, the Lübeck prisoners were moved, together with around 2,900 other officers of 25 nationalities, both air force and army, into a super-camp at Warburg, just outside the village of Doessel. It was a camp that the Germans intended would contain all Allied officers. Size did not mean quality. The Red Cross described Oflag V1B as "much the worst we have seen in Germany". The wooden huts, poorly constructed and leaky, were riddled with bedbugs, lice, fleas, mice and rats. Barrett's own hut had to be fumigated with DDT and the old straw mattresses burnt in the open and replaced before the prisoners were allowed in.

In those early days, there was no electric lighting and the men in each hut read at night by the dim light of a single carbide bulb. The bare clay soil parade ground quickly turned into a sticky quagmire and, more than once, raw sewage overflowed from the ditches that criss-crossed the camp. Nevertheless, morale was high and the prisoners (particularly the army contingent, whom the RAF men mocked with lavatorial humour, calling them "brown jobs" after the colour of their uniform) made determined and defiant efforts to show the strength of their collective spirit. Within ten days of arriving in camp, they put on a variety show. Very quickly, prisoners began to replicate life outside after a fashion, creating an alternative society with all its facilities and amenities, including a gym, chapel, dental practice, barber's shop, tailor's, music room and library.

Their lot was far better than that of the Russian prisoners held in an adjoining enclosure and treated as "*Untermensch*" (sub-human). John Barrett recalled watching the slave gangs being driven out of the camp each day to work. The Allied prisoners passed cigarettes and food over the fence to them when they could. John Buxton wrote to Marjorie, asking with frightening naïvety: "Does anyone send the Russian POWs stuff?" Within a year, more than half of the Russians were dead.

In a matter of weeks, Barrett achieved what Peter Conder had failed to do in seven solitary months among the crowds at Laufen – on walks around the camp courtyard he struck up an acquaintance with a fellow birdwatcher: "John Buxton joined me round and round that circuit in the hopes of seeing birds – any birds at all – a crow or a magpie by the village: a rough-legged buzzard on a hedge-post. For weeks that was about the lot." Barrett had been tipped off about the rough-legged buzzard, described by another prisoner as a "ruddy great crow with snow on its chest". He and Buxton watched the buzzards all winter: "They found something to eat on the snow. What it was we never knew." Otherwise, pickings were lean. Buxton noted: "One can walk 1 hour and see 3 or 4 Crows and a few Sparrows and nothing else at all." He did at least have 300 pages of redstart notes to occupy him, and a droll sense of humour suggested good spirits: "General Fortune* is here; someone sent him a book the other day, The General dies at Dawn."

George Waterston had arrived with Barrett at Warburg as one of the Lübeck contingent. Waterston was among the troops captured in the Mediterranean whom Barrett's RAF wags now dubbed "the Excretas". But he had been taken straight from camp hospital to camp hospital.

A week after arriving at the camp, Peter Conder was writing home to describe an already established routine:

> One of the events of the camp is the morning walk. Breakfast is directly after parade: then the walk begins. Everybody is out, walking up "Lagerstrasse" and down "Kommandaturstrasse" and groups form for few minutes of conversation, then melt away. Towards eleven o'clock the general movement becomes homeward usually with visitors, who come for further chat, exchange of rumours, and, as a matter of course, a brew of tea. They remain for an hour or so, then drift off to soup. The afternoon is spent in sleeping, reading or playing games. The worst part of the day is between tea and "dinner", when everyone is in a flat spin, with insufficient time to settle down to anything. If per chance, you feel an urge to work, the second dining hall is at your disposal, with the dance band or symphony orchestra rehearsing at one end. The main dining hall is the theatre, and, except at meals, is always used for

---

* The same general who had led Conder at St-Valery two years before.

rehearsals. A show goes on every week, and it is hoped that the orchestra will soon perform. Otherwise we get a good laugh from this place. I am most naturally myself.

If Laufen had been a place of cold beauty, Warburg was a mudbath of sociability. Conder had enough self-assurance now to introduce himself to Buxton and Barrett. Buxton had known George Waterston slightly before the war through a short visit to the Isle of May, but did not get to see the hospital patient until November: "I thought he looked more ill than anyone I had ever seen... but he was soon out and about and looking at the birds." Peter Conder also saw Waterston around that time and concurred that the pale Scot had looked exceedingly

Warburg: "an overcrowded hutted camp with non-existent sanitation, all mud in winter, all dust and smell in summer."

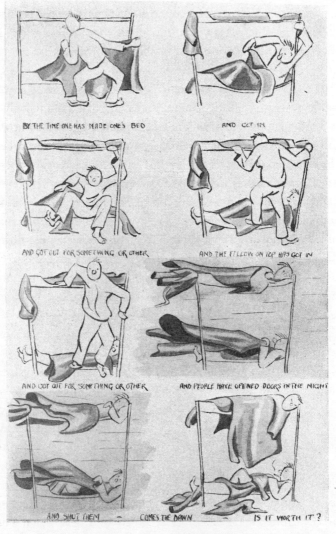

*One prisoner's take on a good night's sleep – a popular cartoon
in the camp magazine.*

unwell, but his later recollections of Waterston's birdwatching endeavours that winter were quite different: "He didn't do much then." Whether he got up and about or not, Waterston accepted his condition with stoicism. Barrett remembered that Waterston's continual complaint at Warburg was that the war had deprived him of the chance to play rugby for Scotland.

Oddly enough, it was Conder, emboldened by his companionable experiences in Biberach, who claimed to have taken the first step towards bringing the four birdwatchers together on a formal basis. On 29th November, he wrote to his father: "Having badgered various people, I've managed to get an ornithological group started; now I am going to sit back and listen to the people who do know something about birds. There are three first class ornithologists here whom it will be useful to know. Luckily, I have kept bird notes since I became a 'Kriegie'." But had Conder taken the initiative? A day later, John Buxton saw himself in the role, writing to Marjorie: "G. Waterston and I are starting a Bird Soc (tomorrow) and hope to do something."

The men met once a month in Buxton's room to record the birds they had seen, and gave talks to each other and anyone else showing any interest. Waterston spoke about the Isle of May. He also recounted the tale of his Lapland birdwatching adventure; it carried a particular resonance when he told of his capture and confinement by Russian border guards. Buxton, the narrator of Skokholm stories, always underplayed his own role: "I suppose I was the leading spirit in the ornithology of prison camps, merely because I contrived to get myself into them before anyone else – I don't know if such a fact is of any interest: it is obviously not a matter of much pride, as it was merely an unhappy accident." Yet he was unquestionably the foundation upon which all their subsequent work was based.

The men did face one insurmountable problem during that winter of 1941–2. Naturalist James Cadbury served out his National Service on the same bleak Westphalian plain some years later. He recalled: "In winter, there were no birds. No robins, no blackbirds. Nothing." No amount of observation or skill could disguise the fact that the camp at Warburg was in the most unpromising position, stuck in the middle of open, almost flat, treeless fields, exposed to bitter, cutting winds across unsheltered ground. An avenue of puny apple trees alongside the road leading down to the nearby village provided the only natural cover.

On 9th December, two days after the Japanese struck at Pearl Harbor, Malaya, Hong Kong and the Philippines, John Buxton wrote to Marjorie to say: "The mud here is about ankle-deep." He also sent a postcard to a pre-war acquaintance, the Swiss ornithologist Fred Schifferli, to thank him for the gift of what was to be an invaluable source of information – Niethammer's *Handbook of German Birds*: "There are very few birds here – 2 crested larks the most interesting." Buxton and his fellow birdwatchers watched the few streaky little larks hopping on the ground outside the wire and listened to their calls. In the book that Buxton had newly received, Niethammer had transcribed the crested lark song as "whee-whee-wheeoo". The prisoners showed a burst of unornithological patriotism and decided that its shrill utterances were actually "God save the Queen."*

---

* Though George VI was on the throne, the last drawn-out note sounded more like "queen".

All that month, Peter Conder was finding what birds he could and the birds – all corvids – were scavenging from their human neighbours. A growing midden of tins and other waste north-east of the camp was gradually drawing in crows, jackdaws and rooks, though the sightings were meagre – a single hooded crow three times in December, a flock of 35 jackdaws on 16th and a rook on 28th December. They were certainly not worthy of any comment in his Boxing Day letter home:

> Christmas went with a swing: – a shocking day – wind, rain, hail and snow. Having saved up for the last month, our cook produced a 7 course breakfast (I felt happy in spite of the weather). We did not want much lunch, tea was excellent – Christmas cake made with pancake powder – went down well. Dinner stumped me, a trifle and jellies were carried over until today. I slept like a king.

Early in the new year, the worst winter of the century in continental Europe became even worse. On the Russian front, temperatures fell to 40 degrees Celsius below zero on five successive nights. Thousands of German soldiers had frostbitten limbs amputated, wounded men froze to death in field hospitals and the Russian army began to push the invading forces back. On the Westphalian plain, John Buxton was feeding blue tits, great tits and a female blackbird on his window sill. Peter Conder remarked: "It is horrible getting up in the morning." The temperature plummeted to minus 25, and though each hut was equipped with a tiny stove supplied with wood and coal that the men "stole" from their captors, ice still formed on the insides of the walls. However, the muddy parade ground was frozen over, making it accessible again, and when it wasn't snowing, the days were sunny.

In the fields beyond the barbed wire, farmers began spreading manure on the fields and where there was muck, there were birds. A fascinated Conder spent a few inconclusive weeks assessing whether animal dung or human dung was the bigger attraction to the increasing numbers of ravenous crows. The birds were ranging widely over the countryside to find unfrozen food. Big beaks dug under animal ordure, or pecked choice scraps from the excrement drawn from the camp latrines and deposited in open-topped chambers just beyond the fence. The rubbish dump grew mountainous and crows picked discarded tins clean. On 14th January, Conder spared his family the finer details: "I am watching crows, these days. I am an object of suspicion and derision. Suspicion from one side of the wire, derision from the other. Derision is getting bored." One week later, he sent an update: "I told you I was an object of suspicion and derision as regards crows. Suspicion had its day, today. I had made a few notes, and was walking on, unaware that all was not well with the world, when I was arrested and escorted to the other side of the wire [maybe the other side of the trip wire, although this is unclear]. My explanations were greeted with laughter, and I was released. It happened just before parade so I kept warm, instead of standing about. This is the second time it has happened and I'm getting quite used to it."

The camp security officer was not convinced, however, and began stalking Conder, who, in eager innocence, carried on with his crow observations, notebook in hand, scribbling furiously, drawing maps. It was all too much. A posse of guards

"A ruddy great crow with snow on its chest" – rough-legged buzzards were among the few birds seen during the winter of 1941–2.

descended on the young lieutenant and grabbed him. His slanting handwriting was barely legible to his countrymen, but its meaning was all too clear to the security officer. This man was planning an escape – punishment: ten days of solitary confinement in the camp cooler.

Carted away, the "guilty" prisoner was disappointed to have his birdwatching interrupted, but he was delighted with his sentence in solitary. Privacy was a valuable commodity that the men bought and sold to each other, taking on fake identities to serve time and enjoy their only opportunity for peace and quiet. In Barrett's words: "No parades, no washing up, nobody to play the saxophone in the next seat, and no arguments whether to have the window open or shut at night."

Over time, and out of habit, German suspicion lessened and eventually died away altogether. Barrett's view was that "after about three months in each new camp, the guards had convinced themselves that we were just another type of harmless idiot that they were paid to watch". The Warburg sentries, still bemused and amused at the lone birdwatching figure, granted him permission to walk close to the perimeter fence, beyond the trip wire, a place where no other prisoners were allowed. But now suspicion came from his own side. Throughout that winter in Warburg, the four men were alone among the thousands of prisoners in their passion for birds. Conder had already overheard one accusing prisoner remark: "That fellow must be mad." Incomprehension was turning to doubt and distrust, and some fellow officers began to suspect that he was a German interloper, planted to spy on the prisoners.

John Barrett, meanwhile, was playing at trying to escape. Warburg was home to two of the war's best-known compulsive would-be escapers, Jock Hamilton-Baillie and, from October 1941, air ace Douglas Bader, who did not let two artificial legs hinder his wanderlust. They led a strong RAF culture of "goon-baiting", non-cooperation and, of course, actively encouraging the other officers in their duty to escape. Those who did not spend all their waking hours plotting were treated with derision. Conder learned to loathe the so-called "tally-ho" men. John Buxton complained that there was no reading room "or only one, and there was usually somebody digging a tunnel from that". The ground under the camp became a honeycomb of tunnels, even though the authorities tried to stop them by blowing them up or filling them with raw sewage from the latrines. The prisoners set up an escape committee to coordinate and vet the numerous proposals for escape. They had given the thumbs up to Barrett and five fellow diggers, who began excavating a tunnel from underneath a store shed. Barrett's team reached as far as the camp boundary, only to dig into the foundation of a support post for the perimeter fence. A temporary thaw brought meltwater running down the post, the roof of the tunnel collapsed and an all too obvious hole was revealed to the ever-alert guards. The escape attempt had been thwarted.

Was Barrett frustrated by failure? He did have especially compelling reasons for wanting to get home that spring: his baby daughter was approaching her first birthday and his first son would be born in June. But risking death was not something that appealed. After the war, he said: "I wanted to get back to Ruth. I didn't try to escape." In any case, he was soon back to birds. He drew inspiration from Buxton's stories of nesting redstarts the previous summer, and so started a nestbox-building project of his own. It remained his own, for though he persuaded the camp authorities to give him scrap wood, and aroused the interest of two of the German officers, he could not cajole his birdwatching companions into sharing the labour of making the boxes, but Buxton did help him put up the boxes on the ends of the huts.

At the beginning of February 1942, Buxton received a letter from fellow poet and novelist Stephen Spender: "The first letter I've had from college... I can't feel sorry for Spender in his noisy room. When I wrote Westward I was in a room with 90 fellows." A greater sense of disengagement with the outside world came when news reached the prisoners that 62,000 Allied troops had surrendered at Singapore to the then all-conquering Japanese. For Conder, gloom was mixed with a grim sense of satisfaction. One of his hut companions had been threatened with disinheritance by his lieutenant colonel father for surrendering at St-Valery. The same judgemental father was among those who capitulated at Singapore.

Though the winter was still at its harshest, Conder continued to beat the bounds: "I've got the same foot trouble that I had in winter 1940, probably through standing about watching these wretched birds." Such was the severity of the conditions, with snow lying on frozen ground, that the crows resorted to coming inside the camp and picking over potato peelings on the kitchen rubbish heaps. The grounds would normally have been crammed with human beings, but, as Conder noted, "numbers of people were permanently in bed to escape the cold".

In the long evenings, he had resumed his advertising career by embarking on a training course: "When I saw the notice telling of this, I didn't say 'What a marvellous opportunity.' I said, 'I've got to do some work.' I really couldn't come back and say that I had been working and yet have nothing to show for it. I can't remember if I have given the impression that I do a lot, and that I will be bringing wads of filled notebooks back. I shan't, perhaps five only and all of it birds and very uninteresting."

On the penultimate day of February came a slight thaw. Conder saw an end in sight for his crow endeavours:

I am working moderately hard on advertising… The rest of my time is spent in watching these crows. I should be able to finish them when they break up for nesting in about a fortnight's time. Then comes the hard and boring work, when, trying to make sense and be accurate whilst going over the notes, I have to wade though over 200 large pages.

Yet there was to be no let-up from intensive birdwatching. The next six weeks were to be among the most memorable in the lives of the ornithologists. Spring migration began and birds that are sedentary in Britain – such as rooks, jackdaws and skylarks – began streaming north-east towards Poland and Russia in huge numbers. Conder captured the excitement of this great passage in his letter home of 19th March:

I've been meaning to write for ages, but strange to say I've been very busy. We thought that we would be very badly off for birds here; we were mistaken. I usually get up pretty early, an hour and a half before most at 7.30 to look at crows. And one morning I saw skylark in large numbers. From then until yesterday, two of us have been gazing in various directions, and the third, lying flat on his back, has been scanning the sky for high fliers. Some of them, rooks mostly, are so high that we cannot see them, and only hear them calling. On the three peak days, over 15,000 birds passed over the camp each day. It beats the numbers seen in some recognised bird observatories, geese and duck excluded. We start watching at dawn and finish at dusk. Then we try and get our notes written up before "Lights Out" at eleven. Even in our dreams we hear the skylarks calling; sometimes we hear other birds, then suddenly realise that we are half awake, and can hear more of the blighters passing. The most spectacular of the lot are the rooks, flying at over a thousand feet, or invisible. Suddenly, they "materialise" – a new scientific expression coined by us. They appear out of the blue, where previously there has been nothing, dive down to a field close by. I am sorry this is such an ornithological letter.

Yours Peter

Skylarks formed the vanguard of the mass migration. On Saturday 7th March, more than 700 flew north-east singly or in small flocks. Two days later, bad weather or thicker snow further north sent birds back southwards, but this time more than three times the original number poured in the opposite direction in flocks of 150 birds or more. Some of the birds came to ground, feeding on a little patch of fresh bare earth exposed after the Germans had blown up an escape tunnel.

The ornithologists quickly mustered themselves into a rota to watch from a slag heap of cinders in a slightly raised corner of the camp, where they had the widest field of view, even though, as Conder remembered, it was none too warm, with snow still on the ground. That evening, as darkness fell, Conder recalled: "Out of the west came, eerily, the sounds of discordant trumpetings, which grew louder and louder, and even when they passed over our heads we saw nothing. They might have been avenging angels for all we knew. Finally, several days later, a party of cranes flew over in daylight – silent until they were over the camp. And then we heard the trumpetings once again and were able to identify the night fliers as cranes."

"I heard their flight calls all day – and I heard them in my dreams that night." – Peter Conder's memory of skylark migration.

By now, rooks and jackdaws constituted the bulk of the mass movement and the men began taking their meals in shifts, ensuring that at least one observer was always present on their lookout post between 7.30am and 7pm. Not quite always. The continuous watch was "only broken by periodical searches of our quarters by the Germans, and by long parades while they were establishing the identity and method of escape of any missing officer".

The numerical zenith came in the middle of the month. On the 14th, the men saw nearly 7,000 skylarks. The following day, Buxton and Conder recorded the daytime passage of 7,659 rooks and jackdaws alone: "Flocks sometimes small, sometimes so large and so high that when the tailend was over us, the leaders had become too small to see... some flew so high that they were only black pinpricks."

On that same evening, Buxton would recall:

> Two of us stood for hours at the door of our hut, hearing the birds flying over: Skylarks and wagtails, ducks of several species, Curlew, Ringed Plover, Golden Plover, Lapwing and at least one party of Cranes. We could neither see them nor estimate their numbers, nor, indeed, identify all the voices we heard; but it was a most moving experience listening in the night to the countless birds calling to keep company in their flocks as, suddenly released from the imprisoning winter, they passed beyond us to the unattainable North.

Buxton was enthralled by the experience: "I've never seen such a spectacle before, for numbers," he told Marjorie. "Three of us (not Waterston, who hasn't got his health back yet) count and scribble all day long!" Painting a too graphic scene, he noted: "I'm out all day on my new 'island' – a heap of cinders in a sea of mud!" Much later came the response: "I hope your new 'island' is exchanged for another one – a pile of cinders in a sea of mud sounds a very dismal story – even though you see exciting birds from it."

An artist by inclination, Conder made a cross-section drawing showing the camp fences at either end and a half-circle sky, with the range of visibility marking where birds could be seen from below. He was illustrating the prisoners' known world.

The following morning, one of the migrants had been brought down to earth – a male skylark, perhaps killed by a predator, they speculated. The men held an autopsy and discovered that the bird had been flying on an empty stomach. On the same day, and for the following five days, John Buxton took no part in the watch – perhaps he had been taken ill. Barrett wrote up each day's records and teased his teacher in his jottings. On the evening of 19th March, he noted provocatively: "Total migrating c800. Very spasmodic watch kept, partly because of rain (mostly laziness)." The next morning, other prisoners held a great debate: "That this House would prefer to be married to Mrs Beeton than Ginger Rogers." Greed won over glamour by 176 votes to 70.

That great pulse of migration lasted 35 days in all. As snow began to melt in the surrounding fields, Conder sent an end-of-season report back home:

> My leisure leads me out of doors for at least twelve hours of the day, from dawn to dusk. Consequently, I am wind-swept and sun beaten, but not only that my left hand is rather swollen with chilblains. Everything, or the worst, is over now. This is the first time I have been afflicted with such things. The amount of notes I have got is really rather stupendous, the only trouble is that it uses up too much paper, in fact I find toilet paper comes in very useful… The bugs are beginning to worry the countryside quite a bit, the noise they make is tremendous and the patterns they form can be seen at good times. Every little helps to brighten a "Kriegie" whether it's birds or bugs. Not that anyone wants brightening. In fact it would need something pretty drastic to damp them.

But what did this huge endeavour amount to? The prisoners were all too aware of the limitations of their study: barbed-wire boundaries meant they were recording only those birds that passed overhead within a narrow front; they could not see birds flying at less than 2,000 feet outside that front. Without binoculars, they could not be sure of what they were looking at above 2,000 feet. And beyond 3,300 feet, they could not see anything at all. There was nothing they could do about the vagaries of weather either – the day after the elation produced by the peak count, Barrett was noting: "Fog up to 1200. The light was so harsh that it was painful to look upwards. Consequently very few main parties seen." Barrett's tally for the day was 3,267 birds, but the actual figure could have been two, three or four times that number. And of course there were the enforced interruptions imposed by their German captors, so that recording was inconsistent.

Yet as the men whiled away the end of winter and the start of spring on their slag heap of cinders, they hypothesised in the long gaps between anything happening, speculated on meanings and patterns within their observations. They consulted the books and papers that friends and families had sent them as lifelines of sanity, to pick over the findings of men who had watched before them and made comparisons.

The *Handbook of German Birds* gave the period of skylark migration as early February in Bavaria and the end of February in East Prussia. But this group of ornithologists was watching them in mid-March. What conclusions could they draw from this? Would these birds be flying to a destination beyond East Prussia? Two years before, the places would have registered only as names on a map. Now they were part of a scientific study that had a purpose. What significance was there in the fact that the bulk of the skylark passage was between

13.00 and 15.00 hours? Had anyone else done any work on skylark migration in central Europe? After all, putting aside their feelings about the nation that held them captive, this land was the cradle of bird migration studies, the birthplace of Heinrich Gätke and Hugo Weigold, the instigators of the world's first bird observatory. In those weeks, far from the maddening crowd down below in the camp, the four men lost their inferior status as POWs. They rediscovered their identities and found solidarity as ornithologists.

And of course, there was the sheer excitement of watching birds:

Immediately north of the camp and easily overlooked from the higher parts of the camp a farmer had dropped piles of farmyard manure about five metres apart on the snow prior to spreading it. These piles were easily visible apparently from a great height because rooks which were flying over at a great height suddenly dived towards them. An individual would close its wings and drop towards the ground. Another would follow and this was enough to stimulate the whole group to follow. Some of these dives were quite spectacular: wings closed and the rook dropped headlong for several hundred feet, before it opened its wings and circled once or twice to slow the descent, before it dived for another 200 feet or more.

This type of descent by waterfowl has been given the name of "whiffling" probably because of the sound their wings make as they dive to the ground. We called it "materialising" because sometimes when they were flying high and silently we failed to see them until several of these

"Descent is mostly with wings half closed, making a bow shaped front." – John Buxton's notes describing rook movements, 15th March 1942.

diving rooks materialised out of the blue sky diving and gliding towards the piles of manure.

Even so, just five years after the war had ended, John Barrett was lamenting a lost opportunity:

Excitement and marvels were in the air, a fresh demonstration that all the stupidities of man could not interrupt the ever turning rhythm of the years. Only four people received this message, though it was plain for all to read. The large birds could not have been more obvious. The storks circling slowly upwards and then gliding gently until they met another up-current on which they could once more climb; smaller parties of cranes with their great night-trumpeting; autumnal flocks of buzzards rising in tighter spirals than the storks' slow sweep; all these sights passed without being seen by over two thousand men with nothing to do but kill time.

The four of us were to blame. We continued unremittingly at our own work without pausing to encourage others to share our joy. "*Sauve qui peut*" [every man for himself] was the motto. We always knew that we might not get any of our notes home. Had we converted only one man each we should have been justified. When we lectured we had no difficulty in interesting the audience. That audience unconsciously longed for reassurance that all things were not bleak and ugly. The chance was lost to show the beauty of simple things.

The lost opportunity would gnaw away at John Barrett for the rest of his life. In the years after the war, he would turn himself into an educator par excellence: he valued the lesson those few months at Warburg had taught him, and was driven to make amends, spurred on to help others appreciate the wonders that had opened his eyes in such unpromising surroundings.

It was probably John Buxton who gave his companions on the mud heap a medium-term goal – publication of their findings in a respected scientific journal, a bulwark against futility. At any rate, should they still be "in the bag" in the autumn to come, there would be the chance of watching the migration south. After all, they had missed most of it the previous autumn.

In early April 1942, towards the tail end of the migration watch, John Barrett was "out" walking near the camp entrance, when he noticed a male and female chaffinch together among six small apple trees, the only trees in the camp. He saw the female gathering nesting material there, but she flew off with it beyond the barbed wire and out of Barrett's view. Nearly two weeks later, while a fellow RAF officer pushed a ping-pong ball around the camp with his nose for 1,700 yards to win a 1,000-Reichsmark bet, Barrett was watching a female chaffinch fifteen feet up one of the trees, binding a twig against a branch. For the next three days, he watched attentively as she made the outer shell of what would be her second nest of the season. The bird continued to build, disregarding the regular surge of noisy men only five yards below and the sound of a (thankfully accomplished) pianist in a neighbouring hut playing solo passages from Beethoven's *Emperor Concerto* (a concert was imminent).

Setting up a nestwatch on a common species was not simply a case of finding something to do. In the first half of the twentieth century, there was an awareness that even basic knowledge of familiar birds was lacking. The pioneering and highly influential ornithologist Max Nicholson had written in *The Art of Bird-watching* (1931): "Casual reading of bird books gives the impression that an enormous amount of observation has been done at the nest, and it is hard for any except specialists to appreciate how serious the gaps still are. So much bird-watching of this kind has been vague, or scrappy, or unsatisfactorily recorded, that even among common species British records on obvious points may be inadequate or non-existent." Mindful of such deficiencies in ornithological knowledge, John Buxton, in all probability, encouraged Barrett to undertake his watch.

Barrett brought out a stool to sit comfortably, but it was too uncomfortable for one security guard who suspected he was involved in some kind of nefarious activity and promptly confiscated his notes. Barrett returned with his stool the next day and every day thereafter for three weeks. His notes were confiscated again and again, but the watcher persisted until the guards gave up paying him attention. He saw the female gather the fluff from prisoners' towels, shreds of paper and wool to line her nest. He watched the pair mating: "With or without first landing beside the female he would very lightly touch her rump with his feet and remain mounted for no more than two seconds." He followed the two-week incubation, put down pieces of ersatz German cheese for the male to pick up for the chicks, and laughed when the chicks refused it.

Barrett's chaffinch watching was not as innocuous as he had led the security guards to believe. By now, the camp's escape committee had cottoned on to the potential for the birdwatchers to act as lookouts. While the bird sat on her nest, Barrett was able to observe the camp entrance, watching who was taking on sentry duties and when. A system of signals was devised so that he could alert another watcher, who stood within view of Barrett, but out of sight of the entrance guards.

One day, rather than taking his notebook to the chaffinch nest, Barrett carried only a couple of sheets of paper. He was hoping for trouble. An orderly had discovered that on that day there would be an inspection of the camp by the International Committee of the Red Cross. Sure enough, two Swiss civilians arrived at the gate, accompanied by a German civilian. The three officials were allowed into the camp and were saluted by the British commanding officer, General Fortune. A few hours later came the changing of the guard and Barrett duly passed on a signal to his fellow officers. Three "officials" – in reality prisoners in disguise – went to the gate, General Fortune gave them an acknowledging salute, the security guard stamped their exit passes and let them out of the camp.

A short while later, the real officials turned up at the entrance and pandemonium broke out among the duped Germans. Barrett was grabbed by infuriated guards and his not-so-precious notes were taken. It was just as he had anticipated. The unrepentant birdwatcher returned to his post the following day, but while he racked up 44 hours of observation during eleven days of fledging, it did not amount to all that much. This was late June when each long day gave a possible sixteen hours of viewing. On only one of those days did he do any watching between 8am and 11am. For a large proportion of that slot, Barrett was sharing a watch with John Buxton's aide-

"The multifarious and frequently tumultuous activities of the three thousand prisoners continually circulating within five yards of the nest did not seem to disturb the chaffinches at all." – John Barrett.

de-birdwatching at Laufen, Richard Purchon. A pair of tree sparrows had taken to one of the nestboxes Barrett had put up in late winter. The two men dedicated more than 750 hours to the birds but all to no avail. Three years later, Barrett would post all of the tree sparrow notes home. It would be a journey with no end, for they never arrived at their destination. Someone, somewhere in Poland or Russia, may still have them.

In this birdwatcher's busy life, John Barrett found time to dig for freedom once more. His hut was one of the least likely places from which to start a tunnel. Stuck in the middle of the camp, it was 120 yards from the perimeter fence – just the spot where the Germans were least expected to look. The men concealed the entrance under their three-foot cast-iron stove, which they hinged so that it could be lifted to expose the tunnel's mouth. Twenty seconds was enough time for them to lower the stove, sweep away the soil, re-light the ever-burning stove and set a pan on to boil. By the time the "ferrets" (security guards whose main role was to ferret out and stop potential escapes) arrived, all would have returned to normal. After four months of digging, the tunnel had passed beneath the growing corn outside the camp. The men were days away from an escape when the heavens opened. A torrential thunderstorm brought down the roof of the tunnel, and so their plans came to naught.

Through the spring and summer of 1942, George Waterston was too ill to do much birdwatching, for his old kidney trouble had flared up again. On one of his few walks around the perimeter fence, he came across a quail that had flown into the barbed wire. Ever the opportunist, he took the bird back to his hut and ate a small but delicious gourmet dish that night.

Though he was largely confined to barracks, sheer determination of will took Waterston out of his pain and the camp surroundings to his spiritual home in the North Atlantic. He filled a notebook with Fair Isle, an account that began like a travel guide: "Although the name 'Fair Isle' is widely known in connection with a distinctive brightly-coloured pullover there are few people indeed who know anything about this little island or its inhabitants." He gave an affectionate insight into the people who lived there: "There are two churches – the Church of Scotland and the Wesleyan Chapel and with a fine impartiality the islanders attend kirk in the morning and chapel in the evening." And he recognised the island's ornithological importance and potential: "The island and its inhabitants are known only to a few enthusiastic bird-watchers who have found in its unique geographical position, an island which is ideally situated for the study of bird migration." Sitting in the melee of a chronically overcrowded camp, Waterston described an island population in terminal decline. The island of St Kilda had been abandoned only a dozen years before – the signs were ominous for Fair Isle, a similarly remote settlement of only about 100 mostly elderly people.

Waterston proposed a plan of action that had perhaps as much to do with his own state of mind as his love for the island. In effect, he was writing a future for himself, creating his own job description.

Suggested Development Scheme

1 Buy the island, or persuade the National Trust for Scotland to buy it, as a Nature Reserve with the establishment of a Bird Observatory under the auspices of the Scottish Ornithologists' Club, with myself as resident warden & factor.

Waterston pumped up the island's ornithological credentials:

Just prior to the outbreak of the second Great War, it was generally agreed by all leading members of the British Trust for Ornithology that… it was high time that a Bird Observatory should be instituted on the most favourably situated island in Great Britain. Bird Observatories have already been started at Skokholm and the Isle of May – equipped with bird traps etc, but neither of these two islands can compare with Fair Isle for the abundance and variety of migratory birds which visit it.

The giddy narrative gave Waterston both a home and a spouse: "I propose to convert the cottage at Pund into a hostel with accommodation for 12 visitors & Resident Warden and his wife." There was something uncannily familiar about the accommodation Waterston envisaged for his future guests: "In the small back bedrooms, double-tier convertible built-in bunks could be used." By comparison, the communal area was portrayed as positively luxurious: "Comfortable cosy chairs & sofa in the sitting room which would also contain a good reference library and all the ornithological records etc." For himself, Waterston desired only austerity: "The Warden's bedroom could be used as a private study-office."

The putative warden laid out the cost of purchasing the island (five shillings an acre) and a possible means: "Raising the money privately within the family at 5% interest." Waterston wrote himself into a role as controller of the islanders' main assets: "Come to an arrangement with all the crofters that I shall purchase their entire output of hosiery at prices to be agreed and that they must agree to do all their marketing through me."

The would-be laird of the isle filled his notebook, then put it aside. A year later, in a different place, he would redraft his proposals and post them to what he hoped would be a receptive ear in Scotland.

John Buxton did not tie himself to studying a single nest, but instead patrolled the camp grounds to maintain daily records of the birds of Warburg. In late May, he told Marjorie: "A ringed plover came here this am!! (probably thinking it was at a sewage farm)." Weeks later, he found a pair of linnets nesting in the safety of the barbed wire.

The poetic muse that had come to Buxton on the grassy slopes of Laufen was absent, stifled by the malodorous conditions. Always an al fresco writer of verse, he could find no inspiration in the heat and dust of the plain, and the ever-present stink of the latrines. He would have to wait for another year to be sent to another camp with more favourable conditions before he would write again.

Early summer was a deeply troubling time for 23-year-old Peter Conder. On 29th May, he wrote to his father: "Birds are very scarce at the moment, and there is very little to do in that line, so I carry on writing my unutterable tripe. It amuses me, it passes the time, and I suppose I learn something from it. The difficulty or perhaps it is a blessing that paper is short." The letter began with content that was far more significant: "Congratulations. I was very pleased to hear you were getting married again. I have been waiting for a letter from you, but so far have not been lucky for some time. You must have been very lonely with everyone whistling off everywhere. I am looking forward even more to the end of the war."

His father was marrying a woman Conder had never met, just four years after the death of his own mother. Furthermore, the teenage sister he had left behind was now a young woman, driving trucks for the Auxiliary Territorial Service, and his younger brother, Neville, declared unfit for service due to a shooting accident that had damaged his hand, was now a trainee architect (he would later join Hugh Casson in a famous partnership that produced, among other buildings, the elephant house at London Zoo). In mid-June, Conder disclosed something of his inner turmoil: "Your accounts of your various doings almost upset my mental stability."

The desperately homesick and confused Conder carried on watching birds… and people. An escape attempt was underway and Conder was persuaded to act as the stooge, the watcher timing the changing of the guard. He would later reflect that he was sent off to a place that was "no good for watching birds". Conder continued making notes and the guards suspected nothing. One evening, the men drew lots to determine who should go under the wire. Conder was picked, much to his secret dismay, for the prospect of crawling through a narrow tunnel and the possibility of being buried alive terrified him.

On the night of 15th June, the escape team made their bid for freedom. Conder endured the ordeal of scrabbling through the tunnel and surfaced on the other side in no fit state to play the hero. Most probably, he was in shock. He vaguely remembered making it to a barn about a hundred yards from the fence. His freedom lasted barely an hour; he simply stayed put until the guards found him and hauled him back inside. The camp cooler was already full, so he was taken away to the local prison at Paderborn. That harrowing evening had its rewards; Conder had ten days of peace and later furnished John Buxton with a snippet which the camp recorder faithfully reported in his notebook: "TAWNY OWL 2 seen by PJC on way to gaol on morning of 16th."

At the end of the month, Conder was back in the camp and refreshed. Perhaps by making it under the wire he had gone through some kind of rite of passage and silenced the "tally-ho" escape obsessives for good. The tone of his next letter home was markedly upbeat: "I have once more taken up birdwatching again with pre-something vigour. My mind was distracted by other things until the day before you got married, and now I sit beneath a Black Redstart's nest for hours on end – weather permitting. I am also writing up my crow notes of last winter. The task looks as though it will take me about 4 months, and in the end I shall learn what I've got to find out next winter."

Conder had found a pair of black redstarts nesting in the roof of a dilapidated barrack hut, where a board had fallen away from the eaves. But if he had hoped to build on the studies into the comparative behaviour of the black and common redstart he had begun at Biberach, he was to be disappointed. Two common redstarts passed through on migration in early April, but none stayed to breed.

Nor was there to be another winter of crow-watching at Warburg. The German authorities were beginning to realise that the British prisoners were becoming uncontrollable in a camp that had experienced more attempted escapes than any other. News reached the men by 24th August: "Well rumour has it that we are on the move again. It is a fairly strong rumour, and the RAF are ready to go. We shall be following shortly. It is of course viewed with mixed feelings. I shall be pleased with a change though the place has grown one or two advantages. My great hope is that I do not lose too many of my ornithological friends. I have had a tremendous education in that line. My knowledge of the technique of watching birds has improved immensely."

The prisoners had one last trick to play. In his short letter of 30th August, Conder revealed more about his proposed destination, but of course said nothing about something of massive significance that he and every other prisoner in the camp knew would be taking place that night: "As I intimated in my last letter we are moving to Oflag VIIB. Rumour has it that it is a better camp with brick buildings instead of wood, and also a good view. This last is a tremendous asset to a camp, as flat cornfields are rather monotonous. We are due to go in a day or two provided that we have no more false alarms. I expect that you will probably have got the news before you get this letter."

That night, the prisoners put into action Operation Olympia, the so-called "Warburg wire job". Forty-six tunnels had produced not a single free man. This time, the plan was to go "over the top". Some seasoned escapers rated it the most daring and successful enterprise of the Second World War. At 10pm, the camp was thrown into temporary darkness by an act of electrical sabotage, a number of home-made stepladders were promptly thrown over the fences and 65 men got over to the other side and into the fields beyond. The next morning, John Buxton and a few others pinned signs to the ladders that read: "Another British evacuation". Three out of 65 made it home to Britain – a high percentage in POW terms.

The rumour machine was correct. Two days later, the four ornithologists were separated. John Barrett and the rest of the RAF contingent were sent east to Schubin. The army men were chaperoned on to a train heading south. Peter Conder was one of the lucky ones who travelled in the luxury of a second-class carriage. A qualified luxury – he spent the night on the luggage rack… and slept soundly all the way to the pretty little Bavarian town of Eichstätt.

EVERY MAN NEEDS A HOBBY

The four men who went birdwatching together at Warburg developed a special bond. Barrett later declared "None of our succeeding trials ever threatened to shake us apart. Never. Our unity was intimate." But what kind of bond did these men have?

An age gap of between six and eight years and status as the ornithological junior made a big difference to 23-year-old Peter Conder. After he was separated from first John Barrett, and then Buxton and Waterston nearly a year later, Conder regretted the loss of his birdwatching advisers, but he was far more troubled by partings from his surrogate family, the barrack hut men with whom he shared the forced intimacies of domestic life. Messmate Ernst Edlmann shared a room with Conder for four years: "Gosh, he took a bit of knowing and I was one of the people who knew him as well as anyone else." Tellingly, Conder would visit his old hut companions with compulsive regularity in the months after repatriation. These were the family that he had come to depend on and he sought reassurance in their company. Deeper friendships with Barrett, Buxton and Waterston only grew in later years as their professional interests coincided and Conder earned a place of parity.

John Barrett had an undoubted affection for Conder, once writing: "He is an exceedingly good person to be associated with", but it was with John Buxton that Barrett developed a strong wartime friendship of opposites, a confident extrovert played off against a nervous introvert. Both highly intelligent men were voracious readers and erudite in a great many topics. Barrett thirsted for knowledge and Buxton was a generous teacher. On Easter Day 1942, he wrote to his wife: "JH Barrett (Sq Ldr)… and I are great friends and I think I've been able to help him to learn more of birds." Three months after the two men were separated, Buxton revealed his feelings of loss in another letter to Marjorie: "I'd love you to exchange news of John Barrett and me through his wife (he was married after I was taken prisoner but has 2 children – one he's never seen). His wife looks very nice and is a farmer's daughter. I hope you'd like her – I shall always want to know him."

George Waterston and John Buxton built a relationship based on shared visions for the future. Each of these modest men had a profound respect for the other's pedigree. Both had about twenty years of birdwatching experience behind them, both had spent a considerable amount of time on islands, both were well connected to the leading ornithologists of the day. And each saw in the other someone who could help hope triumph over despair.

In February 1942, Buxton wrote to Marjorie: "George W and I build many castles for after the war, thickly peopled with birds (esp sea birds that we're not seen for so long)." Fifteen months later, he reiterated the theme: "You'd like him I know, and we are full of plans for after the war." George Waterston told people after he had returned home: "I wouldn't have lasted the war if it hadn't been for birds." He might well have added "and Buxton".

For the rest of their lives, Buxton and Waterston enjoyed a friendship based on birds. In the letters they exchanged, they rarely mentioned anything else. What was it about birdwatching at that time that held the men together?

In his preface to *The Art of Bird-watching* (1931), Max Nicholson tried to encapsulate its appeal:

> Bird-watching is either the most scientific of sports or the most sporting of sciences... As an outdoor recreation demanding knowledge, patience, and skill it comes nearest to shooting and fishing – the avenues by which many bird-watchers have in fact arrived. But it can be practised far more widely than either, and has the advantage, in convenience as well as in ethics, of leaving its quarry unharmed. Its inexpensiveness throws it open to all whose minds turn that way, for it has no bulky paraphernalia and bird-watching rights are not let for money. No occupation of such wide and tenacious appeal can be followed with such promise in so complete a variety of surroundings, from oceans and wild places to the hearts of great towns.

As a hobby, it was definitely seen to be "a good thing", and children were freely encouraged or allowed to roam the countryside at will on their own to explore in a way that would be unthinkable today. Most of the officers in the POW camps were public school-educated and many of these schools would have engendered or fostered their interest through birdwatching societies, or natural history clubs.

We might imagine that in the pre-industrialised farmland of the 1930s and 40s, birdwatching might have enjoyed a boom, for there was a far greater diversity and number of both species and habitats. Skylarks, cuckoos, turtle doves, tree sparrows and grey partridges are just a few of the countryside birds that flourished. There were wild-flower meadows, woods, hedgerows, heaths and marshes that are now lost. But there were substantial drawbacks to put off the putative birdwatcher.

Once he (and it was nearly always he) had left school, there was nothing; he was on his own. The RSPB had fewer than 5,000 members, the British Trust for Ornithology was in its infancy and most county wildlife trusts had yet to be formed. There was no forum for the sharing of information: the bird-watcher in Yorkshire knew nothing of Lancashire. And very few travelled any distance within Britain, let alone abroad. An Essex boy was staggered to hear that his best friend had seen a corncrake on holiday. It wasn't the species that caused the incre-dulity: "Why, he went all the way to Wiltshire!" Most people did their birding on a bike.

There was little cooperation or coordination either. A nation-wide survey of great crested grebes in the early 1930s using amateurs was the first of its kind; a mass observation activity, it drew in only 1,000 people. The typical birdwatcher indulged in the solitary pleasure of taking eggs as a boy, then, having grown out of it as an adult, kept records of sightings purely for his own private enjoyment.

Most off-putting of all was the equipment used to aid, or sometimes impede the hobby. Before the war, there was no such thing as a field guide with helpful pointers to aid identification.

Observers were forced to rely on pictures of birds that looked well stuffed. And indeed they were, for the artists relied on painting taxidermy specimens. Slender birds were shown bloated like bean bags, their colours too pale, since the stuffed models had faded with age and exposure to sunlight. It was a wonder that anyone recognised life from art.

And it was no wonder that Peter Conder failed to identify a black-necked grebe at his first camp at Laufen; his boyhood copy of Coward's *Birds of the British Isles* (an advanced book for its time) showed only a tiny bird in winter plumage. The actual copy that he owned opens to a picture printed out of register.

The pre-war generation also had little of the technical equipment that aids the modern birdwatcher. Few had the poor-quality binoculars (known as field glasses) that were on offer. Fewer still had the bulky seafarers' telescopes that took an age to unscrew and weighed a ton. The watcher would prop it up on the ground, balance the end on his knee, or crush the shoulder of an obliging companion in a bid to keep it still.

The birdwatchers in the POW camps had to work hard, harder than anyone today, studying written descriptions of shape and behaviour to make meaningful judgements of identification. In his wading-bird study at Thorn, Conder would have read that the knot "stands on one leg, its head sunk in its shoulders or with its bill in the scapulars". The other men at Warburg could not be bothered to struggle with their scapulars: birdwatching was just too esoteric, too difficult. And of course, Buxton et al had no binoculars or telescopes to make it any easier for others to join in.

By the time they were captured, the four birdwatchers had already developed their skills and knowledge to such a point that Coward's words in the same work rang true: "Ornithology is progressive. Students of bird-life constantly discover, or imagine that they have discovered, new facts." Isolated from their compatriots, united by the shared language and rules of ornithology, the men drew closer to each other, mutually supportive, bonded by birds.

* * *

For these prisoners, Germany may have been the enemy, but ornithologists were ornithologists the world over. Fellowship went well beyond the barbed wire.

One of their greatest needs was for reference material. These men were using the time they had to fill to undertake what was in fact becoming proper scientific study, and for this relevant books and papers would be essential. They obtained some from ornithologists in Britain, but there were other books and papers that were solely in the possession of their German counterparts. Their requests were more than fulfilled – one man in the capital of Nazi Germany became accustomed to sending his work unprompted to further the prisoners' own studies and the general advancement of science.

That most remarkable and courageous man was an ornithologist in Berlin called Dr Erwin Stresemann, curator of birds at the city's Zoological Museum. Stresemann possessed charisma and a blistering intellect. According to Dr Ian Newton, one of Britain's most respected ornithologists, Stresemann was the very best, "the most influential ornithologist of the 20th century". He was the writer of *Aves*, a groundbreaking work on avian biology, and mentor to many of the leading figures of the next generation, including Konrad Lorenz, Ernst Mayr and India's leading ornithologist, Salim Ali. John Buxton had met the great man at an International Ornithological Congress meeting at Skokholm in 1934. He used the slight acquaintance to appeal from his POW camps for books, journals and bird rings. Stresemann later recalled that he remembered several Buxtons from his visit to Britain, but not John. Nevertheless, with a spirit of fellow feeling, he willingly assisted Buxton, even though metal bird rings would have been especially hard to source. Not only that, Stresemann began a regular and clearly risky correspondence in English with both Buxton and Waterston on ornithological matters. Was there the slightest trace of irony in a letter he sent commenting on the invasion of Germany by the advancing collared dove?

Stresemann wrote cheerily to Waterston: "We had a most successful meeting of the Deutsche Ornithologische Gesellschaft a month ago, attended by about 140 members and many guests. It lasted for three successive days (including an excursion to see birds of prey)." All this on the day the Red Army launched a fresh offensive against the German forces.

Throughout the war, Stresemann played a dangerous game running with the wolf. The commander of a German regiment in occupied Crete took time out from shooting partisans to shoot birds and sent descriptions of his finds to Stresemann to have them identified. It wasn't always possible to do so, and following invitations, the curator made what must have been somewhat uncomfortable visits to the island. His first trip was in the summer of 1941 just after Germany had overrun the island. He returned in early 1942, accompanying the commander and his cronies in a duck shoot. Stresemann then turned the trips to

DEUTSCHE
ORNITHOLOGISCHE
GESELLSCHAFT
BERLIN N 4, INVALIDENSTR. 43
FERNRUF: 42 71 86
POSTSCHECKKONTO: BERLIN 308 41

BERLIN, DEN 2. August 1943

Lieut. George Waterston
British Prisoner of War Nr. 3695

Oflag. VII B

E i c h s t ä t t

Dear Sir,

I have been greatly surprised by getting your Notes on the birds of
Crete together with your interesting letter. Until now I had no idea
that in present times our ornithologiscal journals, the Journal für
Ornithologie, Ornithologische Monatsberichte and Vogelzug, would be
of some use to Members of the B.O.U.

Your List looks rather complete considering the district in which
your observations have been made, and some of your records are certainly worth publishing. Emberiza hortulana on 25.3. looks extremly
early. In 1942 and 1943 the birds of Crete have been studied by several German ornithologists, who also did some collecting, and a
first report by Dr. Niethammer w... soon be out in print. One of
our best known bird photographers, Horst Siewert, has made a marvellous film on Birdlife in the White Montains, including Lammergeier
and Griffon Vultur, which I hope you and your comrades will be able
to see one day.

I have not seen the Journal of Animal Ecology since 1939, and therefore did miss your paper on the Fulmar. Neither had I any opportunity of reading Mr. John Buxtons paper on the Oystercatcher publ. late
in 1939. Ornithologists will have a hard Time after the war if they
want to read all the important stuff published in the mean time,
across the water. Have you seen my review of Herr Ruiters paper on
the breeding biology of the Redstart? I wish you would add to this.

I shall try to send you a copy of the Ibis for Jan. 1939 hoping that
you may be able to return ist before long to the library of the Deutsche Ornithologische Gesellschaft. Its our only copy, you know. The
Ibis for 1940 ist not represented in any of our libraries; I saw it
at the Paris Museum.

It would be very nice if we could remain in touch with another. With
my best wishes

Yours sincerely

Erwin Stresemann

*A letter to a British soldier in English – written within a mile of
the Gestapo headquarters in Berlin.*

his advantage by producing a paper on the birds of Crete. But like any professional ornithologist, he knew his paper would be given extra validity by the inclusion of records from others who had studied birds on the island. It was only natural, therefore, that he should turn to a British soldier and ornithologist who he knew had been birdwatching on Crete (when he wasn't fighting Stresemann's own countrymen). George Waterston posted his records to Stresemann and the latter replied with a letter of thanks, adding: "It would be very nice if we could remain in touch with another [sic]."

In due course, Stresemann published his paper, translated as "A survey of the birds of Crete and bird migration in the Aegean", in the *Journal für Ornithologie*. Not only did he include Waterston's findings, he had the courage and audacity to acknowledge the officer's help within the paper, not once but twice. The first covert mention of G Waterston sits within the category of records in earlier years, the second a frank note of thanks to (in translation) "Lt Waterston, who thoughtfully and kindly put together the ornithological observations he had made on Crete on the south side of Suda Bay during the spring of 1941". Of course, those in authority might have scanned over the name and read in the abbreviated rank Lt the word *Leutnant* and thought nothing of it. Stresemann was very clever. And so George was able to boast for the rest of his life that he was the only serving British officer to contribute to a German scientific paper in wartime.

Eventually, the net began to close around the Berlin professor. He was given a warning about corresponding with British soldiers in English and, very sensibly, he heeded that advice.

In 1945, as bombing intensified over the city, Stresemann somehow requisitioned a truck and a platoon of soldiers, and supervised the transfer of the precious contents of the Zoological Museum to the safety of a country estate. He sat out the rest of the war, his health badly affected by the famine of that year.

Shortly after his return to England, John Buxton received a letter from Stresemann:

> I beg to assure you how greatly I welcomed the opportunity of helping a brother ornithologist to overcome the mental strain of being a prisoner of war as far as I could, and how much I delighted in the correspondence with

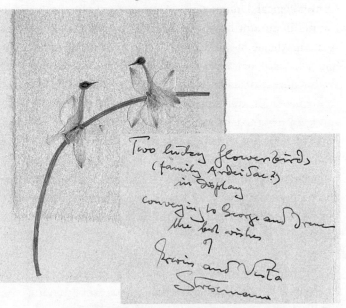

Cover and back of the last card sent by Stresemann to the Waterstons, two years before he died.

you, who had such a broad view of everything relating to
the thorough study of life history.

In July 1945, Waterston wrote to Buxton: "I feel that we
should make an effort to do something for Stresemann in view
of the many good turns he did for us in Eichstätt." However,
aiding a German in an occupied zone would have been very
difficult. More than a year later, the two men resolved to invite
Stresemann to the International Ornithological Congress to
be held in Edinburgh in 1947. At that time, travel abroad by
a German was only possible by written invitation from the
host country, and so the two ex-prisoners supplied the British
Ornithological Union with a letter describing the help that
the Berlin curator had given to them in captivity. Baxter and
Rintoul, the joint presidents of the Scottish Ornithological
Club, backed their application. But a vindictive member of the
BOU concealed the letter from the rest of the committee and
so no invitation was issued. Ashamed and infuriated, Buxton
promptly resigned from the BOU. Stresemann accepted the
news of rejection with dignity. "It is always difficult in these
affairs of the heart," he replied.

Stresemann maintained his friendship with Buxton and
Waterston for the rest of his long life. In 1970, two years
before his death, he sent a card to George, containing a wistful
message:

If I was still in my sixty's year
I would fly to the birdwatchers' isle called Fair
But I am eighty
So geht's leider nicht mehr. [sadly, so it goes no more]

* * *

A younger ornithologist called Günther Niethammer, curator of birds at Bonn Museum, had already established massive ornithological credentials by producing three definitive reference volumes on German birds, the *Handbuch der Deutscher Vogelkunde*. It became a birder's bible for the men in their various camps. In February 1944, following up on Stresemann's paper on the birds of Crete, Niethammer sent a copy of his own newly published paper on the subject to John Buxton.

Except that he didn't. The inscription on the flyleaf reads "Lieut. John Buxton, mit besten Gruss". But the scrawled signature underneath does not belong to Niethammer. The paper was signed by his boss at the museum, one von Jordaens. Where was Niethammer? Very likely he was away on one of his regular spells of duty guarding the inmates of Auschwitz concentration camp.

Niethammer's story is one of extraordinary moral complexity. A card-carrying member of the Nazi party, he claimed friends had persuaded him to pass over the ordinary Wehrmacht for a position in the elite force of the Waffen SS. Niethammer found himself posted to Auschwitz, where he said he was only ever a guard patrolling outside the barbed wire. And what could he do there in his spare time but watch birds? The *Kommandant* actively encouraged Niethammer's extra-curricular activities.

While ten Polish civilians were being deliberately starved to death inside the camp, Niethammer heard a nightingale singing outside. He noted eight curlews seen and heard over an area of ponds on the day Zyklon B was used to gas Russian prisoners. He published his records from the spring and summer of

1941 in a paper of observations on the birds of Auschwitz. Two years after the war ended, Niethammer's guilt at his passive complicity had driven him to offer himself up voluntarily to the occupying authorities, while countless others chose to hide their past. He served three years in a Polish prison for his security role at the concentration camp, but always maintained he had acted under duress.

Niethammer held positions of authority in German ornithology right up to his death in 1974, but grieved that British ornithologists never answered his letters. Though Niethammer never knew it, Waterston felt sympathy for him, but for whatever reason, appeared not to have communicated his support. Writing to Buxton on hearing of the German's release in 1950, Waterston commented: "Niethammer seems to have had a tough time of it and it is good to hear that there are people like Shaw who are doing their best to alleviate the beastly suffering of some of these unfortunates." JE Shaw, the British military intelligence officer who had formally taken Niethammer's surrender and listened to his story, was convinced that his crime was merely to have been astonishingly naive. Shortly after meeting up with Niethammer following his release, Shaw wrote to Waterston: "Again he takes pleasure in ordinary things. His wife. His work. Green fields. Birds singing."

NEAR TO PARADISE

"Now I am far from the bombs' whine, sirens' shriek,
Far from these English hours of pride, not fighting still,
Nor at peace, but useless, inert, for this time dead."
John Buxton, "Lines on re-reading Robert Bridges'
'The College Garden' in 1917".

On a sunny 2nd September 1942, the army officers were
marched into a broad Bavarian valley where the mighty Danube
had flowed millions of years before. The beautiful, blue Danube
had long since altered its course, leaving a little reed-fringed
tributary, the River Altmuhl, to run apologetically through
the valley bottom. Meadows and corn fields on one bank rose
up to a limestone bluff covered in bushy undergrowth and
further along, a forest of beeches, oaks, spruces and larches.
On the opposite bank sat the attractive, largely eighteenth-cen-
tury town of Eichstätt. At the eastern end of the town, an old
cavalry barracks, terraced into the hillside, had been converted
into a POW camp. The military authorities had, for once, built
extra huts out of brick instead of wood. And after the bleak,
exposed, empty plain of Warburg, Oflag VIIB was filled with

trees. Cherry, maple, sycamore, birch and ash trees were sprinkled through the spacious grounds of a camp that boasted a football pitch and vegetable gardens, in addition to the obligatory parade ground. A great double avenue of mature limes ran along the southern boundary.

Written some time after their arrival, Conder's notes capture some of the prisoners' incredulity at what they encountered: "As we walked into the camp at Eichstätt in Bavaria on September 2nd 1942, we thought that at last the rumours of a luxury camp had come true. At first sight, especially to those of us who watched birds, it seemed as near to paradise as possible in a prison camp." Conder looked across the river to the forested slopes opposite and was reminded of the Surrey heathlands of his childhood in an area of brown-tipped bracken, young birches and oak. Simultaneously, John Buxton gazed in the same direction and wrote to Marjorie to say it looked like Oxfordshire's Christmas Common.

The next day, the men were ordered down a ramp onto the football pitch to endure the first of many tedious, time-consuming searches. As they lined up, a charm of some 60 goldfinches flew overhead, most of them young birds. In fact, there were young birds everywhere, the harvest of a rich breeding season. The three birdwatchers began to search the trees for evidence of nesting, but the foliage was too dense to see anything much. However, the very act of looking had its benefits – Conder spotted a wryneck, a small, cryptically coloured woodpecker of some rarity back home. Three weeks later, John Buxton told Schifferli, his Swiss ornithologist friend: "I have moved to a new camp now where there are more resident birds than at the last – Orioles, Black and Common Redstarts,

Chiffchaff (still singing) & Red-backed Shrike. There has been a Green Sandpiper once or twice too." Other prisoners with only a passing interest in birds became infected with the excitement and passion and began to quiz the expert trio about how many species they might see the following spring. Guarded for fear of later ridicule, the men gave a low figure. But even the estimates that they shared privately with each other were to be exceeded.

Initially, the birdwatchers' enthusiasm for their surroundings was tempered by the behaviour of an overzealous camp commandant. The only one of the German officers not to have served on a battlefield, Oberst-Leutnant Blätterbauer made up for a lack of military nous with an unhealthy relish for installing strict discipline on his new charges. The order came through: "Officers will wear overcoats properly buttoned up when on appel [parade]. The reading of books on appel is forbidden and will be punished. By order of Oberst-Lieutnant Blätterbauer, Oflag VII-B."

One of the officers, Captain The Earl of Hopetoun, caught the mood on parade:

> Parade "Shun!" (British order, and therefore obeyed) –
> Stand at ease – Blatters takes the salute with a click of his
> podgy legs and walks threateningly towards the leading
> ranks. "Blimey, he's inspecting us. Yoo-hoo Blatters, you
> old sod. How are we looking?"

Blätterbauer increased the number of parades and the men responded by turning up in scruffs, sometimes without shirts on. Another order came through: "Prisoners must attend appel wearing shirts." Every one of the men stood to attention at the next roll-call wearing shirts… and nothing else. Blätterbauer's fellow officers sniggered and the rod of iron was broken.

As summer turned into autumn, Conder was in an almost buoyant mood. On 11th October, he wrote home:

> I plan to do about 12 hours mental work a week. At present I am working out the average height of crows with the wind coming from the 8 points of the compass at different speeds. Having found out as much as I can about that, I check up on the behaviour of the crows in the above conditions, and draw my conclusions which as you can imagine are usually very similar to that well-known fruit – the lemon. But it's good exercise, and rather strangely it intrigues me, rather than boring me. I often wonder if I should write a paper on the behaviour of the flies on the boards of the bed above me.

The birdwatchers were also in a practical mood. Perhaps they found old floorboards or they were given bits of broken bunk beds. However they obtained their wood, they set to making and putting up nestboxes around the camp. A collective effort saw 26 in place by the start of the following breeding season.

Events in the world outside were about to have a dreadful impact on one of the birdwatchers' lives. Every night, an officer from each room would crowd round the single illicit radio in the camp to hear the BBC news at 9pm, then return to his hut and recount all he had heard to his fellow prisoners as they lay in their bunks after lights-out. The main story one night was of direct relevance to the men. Hearing that

German captives taken in a commando raid on the Channel Island of Sark had apparently been shot while their hands were tied, Hitler ordered a reprisal. He demanded that all Allied troops captured during an abortive attack on Dieppe the previous month – where Canadian soldiers had supposedly roped German prisoners together – should be manacled. The men – mostly Canadians – had been spread around three POW camps, Eichstätt being one of them. They were promptly handcuffed. The British public was outraged at such a blatant breach of the Geneva Convention. On 25th October, John Buxton sought to reassure his wife Marjorie: "I am still unmanacled, and you are not to worry about me. In the long run all this may do us some good as it is at least waking people up to our position, about which they have always been so smug until now." Yet Marjorie Buxton was right to be concerned. Churchill had ordered a retaliatory manacling of German POWs. Hitler pursued the tit-for-tat with compound malice and demanded that three times as many Allied prisoners should be cuffed. A few days later, a second round of shackling took place and John Buxton was one of 250 in the camp made to wear handcuffs with short chains between them. Every morning, a guard would come into the room and bind the wrists of the unfortunates. And the men would be left chained in the manacles for the whole day until they were unlocked at night.

Denied his liberty and now deprived of the right to move freely, Buxton's state of mind can only be guessed at. The man who had never had a proper job "celebrated" his 30th birthday in chains. Outwardly, at least, all the men affected showed great spirit.

On 4th November, Conder wrote home: "The handcuffed boys are quite cheerful, after they have got used to it." They were even more cheerful when one of their number discovered how to pick the handcuff locks. In the barracks at least, they could go unfettered as long as there were no guards about.

Buxton soon immersed himself in academic endeavour. Appointed one of the librarians to the camp (as he had been at Laufen), he and his fellow bibliophiles began to accumulate and distribute books to the knowledge-hungry men. By the end of the war, there were 15,000 books in the library. Buxton stretched his considerable talent for languages too by learning Welsh from a major in the Welsh Guards, and translating Norwegian books and Old Norse sagas. He also translated the German words of Mozart's *Magic Flute* for a winter musical festival that would be conducted by Lieutenant Wood, a future director of Glyndebourne. At the performances in February, the camp choir sang a piece composed especially for the occasion, and posted to Bavaria by Benjamin Britten.

The magic flute in Mozart's opera was played by accountant Maurice Waterhouse, Buxton's hut companion and a fellow graduate of New College. Waterhouse's pedigree as a great-nephew of Poet Laureate Robert Bridges was largely irrelevant, but his role as a willing watcher with boundless patience would serve the ornithologists well over the next two nesting seasons.

Buxton rediscovered his own poetic muse, pouring out thirteen poems in eight days. He sent his work home to Marjorie and he asked her to find a publisher for a selection of these and the poems he had written at Laufen. A year later, they saw publication under the title *Such Liberty*.

"I hope to get my photograph soon. I warn you it will be shocking. I was completely unprepared." – a long-haired Conder posing with his POW number.

Buxton longed for his absent birdwatching friend: "I miss John Barrett – if you wrote to his wife at Cringleford near Norwich we might exchange a little news." The two men's wives would ensure that the separated POWs kept in some kind of contact for the next two years. And of course, hindered though he was by his manacles, Buxton went outside to watch birds, setting up a new list – Birds of Eichstätt.

* * *

Peter Conder's birdwatching that autumn and winter was paying dividends, especially when he looked out to the reed-beds by the river:

> In the evening they were dark and bent with the weight of
> two or three thousand roosting starlings. One morning I
> got up early and as I looked over the mist-covered valley,

it was suddenly filled with them as they rose from the reeds... The camp seemed to be the centre of a roosting area, because not only did the starlings gather on the north hill and then, just before sunset, sweep over the camp and dive into the reeds from fifty to a hundred feet with twisting bodies and wings, but yellowhammers, greenfinches, goldfinches, chaffinches, house and tree sparrows gathered in the limes... all these as they approached flew very excitedly, swerving from side to side and then diving down, again swerving, opening and closing their wings, calling vigorously.

For all his enthusiasm, at Eichstätt, just as at Warburg, Conder remained very much the office junior. Buxton and Waterston carried authority, not just because they were experienced, older birdwatchers who had now entered their thirties; they had also learned before the war from men vastly more knowledgeable and experienced than themselves. In later years, Conder would write appreciatively: "It was from them that I learned to be more critical and exact in my recording of bird habits." Largely self-taught and willing to be self-critical, the 23-year-old Conder was nevertheless confident and honest in his uncertainty. He could make notebook entries so frank they would make any birdwatcher wince: "I regret to have to admit a gross error. In fact all the entries which refer to the wren above are in reality hedge sparrow"; and "3 large birds flew S over the camp at c300ft; I have not got the slightest idea what they were." But there was the occasional little triumph where the pupil scored over a teacher: "Three birds in the limes – I thought them to be siskins at first, but GW appeared and said that it sounded like a redpoll." Unconvinced by the contrary opinion of his "superior", Conder left the siskin record in his notebook. Six days later came vindication: "EJMB [Buxton] throws some doubt upon the redpolls saying that this morning one of them was definitely a male siskin."

There is no question that, for Conder, Buxton was the highest authority – in everything. Notes made on an early spring walk show both innocent ignorance of plants and the faith of the young man in his mentor:

> I made an expedition in search of flowers this morning and was agreeably surprised with what I found. I started off with violets on the bank immediately S of block 2. Below the path was a dandelion in flower. Between the trip wire and the rabbit fencing under the limes were many patches of the pale blue flowers of speedwell… To the E of the camp directly under the trip wire is a patch of pale purple flowers at the moment about 6" high, which may possibly be dead nettles… Later on I was taken round by EJMB & PS [an unknown name] and they pointed me out various things. Firstly that one of the spurges was a pink stonecrop, the one that did not have light coloured petals in the centre. The other was a sun spurge.

Flowers were an occasional bright distraction from what in early spring 1943 was fast becoming the main event. The most verdant of all POW camps was now attracting an enormous number and variety of birds, some passing through on migration, many more preparing to breed within and around the camp: "I put up nestbox 19 in front of block 2 instead of by the garden entry abort [toilet] at 1855 last night. GW says that a great tit went inside this box and was 'knocking up shelves' in it at c0700 this morning." On the same day, house sparrows and starlings were carrying nesting material into the clock tower and a blue tit was building in one of the nestboxes. Conder, however, had his sights set on another more glamorous species: "This summer I rather want to specialise on the Swallow on rather a bigger scale," he wrote home.

John Buxton was also in optimistic mood about the here, now and future: "Writing this sitting in the sun, while a chaffinch sings above my head, and another not far off and a yellowhammer and now and then a lark… I'm glad Ron [Lockley] is active about Nat Parks and reserves and I think we'd like to work in that, wouldn't we? I saw a flock of Lapwings yesterday pm from my bed, which cheered me up a lot. I do love them."

He now had another more tangible cause for celebration. In the spring, his shackles came off. The guards at Eichstätt had grown tired of administering the daily act of wanton cruelty. A far less onerous daily ritual now began. The guards handed the prisoners their manacles in the morning and the prisoners hung them on pegs for the day. At night, the guards returned to collect them again. Duty was observed, honour was satisfied and for the next few months, until November, when the order was finally rescinded, the two sides kept up their clanking charade.

On April Fools' Day, Buxton received a report of "a bird with a red breast and a white mark as big as a shilling on its head" on the wire behind Block 2. This was no joke – the description was

A rough sketch at Eichstätt, showing redstart Nestbox 17 (in the tree on the left) that was attacked by wrynecks.

so precise that Buxton knew it had to be a male redstart. But the experience of Laufen had taught him to suspect that a bird this early would be only a passage migrant. Sure enough, more male birds came and went over the next few days. Snow fell on the eighth and, perhaps not expecting much, Peter Conder spent most of the following day lolling around on his bunk, only getting up to open a window to check the temperature. A chiding Buxton called him outside at 5pm and told him he had been rather lazy. There on the grass among some fresh mole-hills were a male redstart, four black redstarts and two male wheatears. Conder needed to raise his game.

Indeed he did. Two days later, great tits began building in two nestboxes. Nobody rushed to watch them, but Richard Purchon settled down the next day in front of a lime tree where a chaffinch was building her nest. More than likely, he hoped to build on the studies that the now-absent John Barrett had carried out on nesting chaffinches the previous year. Six more days passed before a male redstart fluttered up to sing at two nestboxes in the hope of luring a female (should one appear). And that same evening, Conder recorded: "Peter McCall showed me the beginnings of a Goldfinches' nest in a small elder tree outside my staircase. It is in a very frequented area, as people frequently stand beneath it and often climb it to watch a football match. The nest is c10' from the ground in a fork of twigs."

"She was collecting spiders' webs from under the eaves of the sentry box." – Conder's extraordinarily observant watch of the goldfinch.

Conder's time had come. Buxton had freely shown him the redstart notes he had made at Laufen. Conder had studied and learned from them. The black redstart nest that he had watched at Warburg, albeit for only a couple of weeks, had also given him a sense of what to do. And now here was a pair of pretty birds nesting 30 feet from his front door and visible from his barrack room window: "On the morning following the discovery of 'A' nest I sat down on my stool, propped my back against the music-room wall, and watched and wrote." Two days later, Buxton wrote mischievously to Marjorie: "A Goldfinch nesting – tell John B that Peter Conder is rivalling him with this."

Conder's vigil was an extraordinary feat of intense and sustained observation. He saw the female goldfinch gather material for her nest, saw her pluck strands of cotton from the barbed wire washing lines that prisoners had used to hang up their towels, saw her on the rubbish dump pulling out the discarded strips of paper from Red Cross parcels, saw her teasing out spiders' webs from the eaves of the sentry box to bind her nest together. He watched her head bob up and down as she weaved the strands together, watched her garland the cup inside with the blue heads of forget-me-not and bright yellow alyssum flowers.

And without binoculars he saw courtship behaviour that no other ornithologist had recorded before: the two birds sitting on a branch barely an inch apart, kissing beak to beak in rapid succession; sometimes the male pressing his closed beak into the female's open mouth. He saw mock feeding and actual feeding of the female by her suitor. He sat in horror as men crowded on the bank three deep to watch football, rugby and softball matches, sometimes grabbing onto the elder trunk and shaking it in their excitement, or even climbing up the branches for a better view. But the female sat tight on her nest, above the hubbub, incubating her eggs.

Conder himself, sitting in such a public position, started to become an object of interest. As he related to his father: "Practically the whole camp comes at regularly spaced intervals to stand and look up at it and not only that but will keep on asking me questions when I am trying to look at the bird, or write down what I have seen."

For all the few moments of pleasure, there were hours of tedium. Conder had acquired old cash books in which to make his notes, and as the weeks rolled by, his frustration and desire for fresh stimulation began to show: "Feeling exceedingly bored I began watching," he wrote at the start of one afternoon session. He began to invest the little birds with personality to relieve the dullness of repetitive note-taking: "The chicks sitting low on the nest. One chap stretches neck and looks around." And these were long spring days – Conder took to his stool every morning around 7.30. One of his best friends in camp, a Worcestershire solicitor called Bertie Evers, gave him an hour off in mid-morning to stretch his legs and do his chores. For Evers, it was a welcome distraction: "I often used to watch and take notes when he was off duty; it was a very exhaustive affair. As I was on an escape project at the time and the tension was inclined to build up, this was a very useful pastime, which demanded concentration on so beautiful an object as a goldfinch."

Another messmate by the name of Ashe relieved Conder for an hour late in the afternoon. Otherwise, he sat fixed to his seat until 8pm every day, breaking only to come inside and take his meals at the barrack room window. But still he watched. The male goldfinch flew to the nest to feed his brooding female: the men in Block 2 took dinner to the duty ornithologist.

Every evening he returned to his bunk to write up his notes. No wonder one entry reported: "I overslept badly and so did not get out until 0800." That day, he managed a watch of only twelve and a half hours.

He had reason to feel a little aggrieved. On the day he began his watch, John Buxton's bird sang. He counted his redstart – as yet without a mate – performing nine songs per minute. The senior ornithologist had begun his watch in earnest and he had managed to attract sixteen men to assist him, among them George Waterston. While Conder sat alone at Nest A, Buxton had a nice little shift going. Of course, Buxton had had two years to plan cooperative observation, and, no doubt, had courted his assistants well in advance. He had also done his thinking:

> The number of watchers in 1943 was in itself sufficient guarantee against any preconceived ideas destroying the accuracy of observation; and where so many, of whom some had seldom or never before watched birds, are in agreement upon what they see, it may be agreed that what they recorded is what occurred.
>
> Purposely I did not inform my fellow-watchers of what I thought was happening from day to day, so that the notes cannot be said in any way to reflect my own ideas derived from observation in 1941.

Buxton and his team saw the female redstart arrive on 21st April, to be serenaded with an aria lasting twelve minutes. A day later, Richard Purchon's chaffinch watch came to a premature end when the birds deserted. On the 24th, he told Conder that a pair of goldfinches was raiding his erstwhile chaffinch nest for leaves and twigs. The next morning, Buxton's female was herself gathering nest material and the male – the best singer Buxton ever heard – fell silent.

Buxton's determinedly scientific written-up account does not record the distinctly unscientific event that followed. On the morning the female laid her first egg, a wryneck arrived at the nest. This little woodpecker, twisting its head sinuously like a snake, habitually destroys the nests of other birds before making them its own. The men were not prepared to let nature take its course here with eighteen days of effort behind them. Maurice Waterhouse picked up a handful of gravel and began pelting the wryneck with tiny stones. Though his hand was just six inches from the bird, the wryneck held its tenacious grip and the redstarts deserted. It was not the end of Buxton's watch, however. Twice the redstarts would be evicted by wrynecks and twice the male would fly to another box and sing to entice the female to make a fresh start. Half an hour after the second nest, complete with four eggs, was destroyed, the male was singing again.

Now it was George Waterston's turn to disappoint Conder. Waterston was captivated by the bold usurpers and began to watch the wrynecks, drumming up a new team of thirteen willing assistants.

Conder, meanwhile, was up to his ears in goldfinches. He took a short break from his watch one day to make an

Conder recorded details of goldfinch nesting behaviour that no other observer had ever seen. And all this without binoculars.

inspection of the camp and estimated that at least eight pairs were breeding all at once. At last, assistance came. Four men took a stand within sight of two lime tree nests, where they could watch "as simultaneously as possible" until emerging leaves rendered further viewing impossible. Conder trimmed back the leaves around the nest in another tree and, much to his dismay, caused the incubating birds to desert. Another nest was wrecked when firewood seekers pulled down twigs for their barrack room smokeless heaters. Conder took particular care with his original nest, pruning back the leaves of the elder one at a time, making sure that the female stayed sitting. But it was still difficult to see exactly what was happening, so the men resorted to artificial aids:

> At 0915 an examination of the nest was carried out with the usual aid of the handcart and a stool and a mirror. As regards the nest, the inner cup was clean, but the top of the rim and outer rim were filthy as can be seen in the case of the outer rim from the ground. The chicks were sparsely covered with tiny but complete feathers. The primaries of the wings were prominently developed and the wings showed the gold markings very clearly. Consequent upon a TOO CLOSE examination by DW* one of the chicks took flight and performed a steep glide to the ground. He was picked up and restored unhurt. He uttered a shrill tzie note on the ground. [and then in a different hand] Note for future examinations SMG* is to provide chicks with parachutes.

Disaster almost struck Conder's main nest on 25th May:

> Of animals, only the cat that lived in my staircase in block 2 only thirty yards away from the nest and had littered in the loft of the music room caused me a tremendous amount of bother. Luckily it did not find the nest until five days before they were due to leave. At feeding time a crowd was apt to gather beneath the

---

* Derek Woodward and Simon Green, two of Conder's watchers. Woodward later became related to Conder by marriage.

tree to watch the parents, and this might have hindered the parents from seeing the cat. At any rate the hen was feeding the young, the cock was calling from the top of the tree, and the chicks were shrieking as loudly as they could. Suddenly the black cat was halfway up the tree with its ears back. Just as quickly one of the bystanders had it off the tree, and away, with tremendous shouts and stones following it. I was too shaken to do anything but gape. I watched the cat very carefully after that until the cat's owner and myself rigged up a formidable barbed-wire entanglement which proved completely successful.

Fledging day for the goldfinches came, and once the first couple of birds had taken their faltering leave of the nest to the outer branches of the elder, word got round the camp. By midday, a huge crowd had gathered around the tree. One by one, the little birds lifted off from the nestcup and settled onto a nearby perch, but, rather comically, when the adult birds came down to feed them, the babies would jump on top of them, just as they would jump on top of their siblings when food was brought to the nest. Riding their parents' backs, their little wings whirring, it looked for all the world as if they were trying to mate with them. The curious onlookers cheered at seeing these little birds gaining their freedom.

Unquestionably, bird fever had caught a sizeable proportion of the prison population. It was not just that 30 or so bird-watchers would be following a daily routine all around them; birds were visible everywhere:

Young yellowhammers are all over the camp, and one was being fed by Block 1 people. If a finger was placed a foot from it and a foot from the ground, the young bird hopped on it. When the hand was raised to c4 or 5 feet, it flew off and landed again, only to repeat the performance if the finger was offered it. It was fed c 10 beetles, then flew off of its own accord.

Men could not avoid seeing birds, even indoors. Conder noted:

A male swallow has been investigating the hall and landing on my staircase. [He] comes thro' the door every time. He comes in, hovers round with slow wing beats, tail hanging down, settles on the pipes containing electric wires, now glides, settles on the lampshade. From its perch it looks around, once turned right round. It hovers very slowly, going up and down stairs and flies out by the upper landing window.

The nesting swallows also attracted the attention of Richard Purchon and he set up a team of four to make observations covering one hour out of every three. Lacking the real thing, he and Buxton set to making home-made bird rings. Somehow, Buxton was able to ring the swallow chicks in the nest, and the little bands stayed on all the way to Africa and back. A year later, seven of these babies would return to the camp.

The birds in Purchon's first nest nearly came to a sticky end when the little mud cup fell off the rafter and broke open on a locker below. The chicks set up a great cheeping from their new location; the adults flew back to the rafters to feed them, but could not locate their vociferous offspring. John Buxton found a condensed-milk tin, lined it with cotton wool, stuck the babies inside and placed it up on the rafters. The adults promptly returned with food and the chicks were saved.

Conder, meanwhile, had walked round the corner to mount watch on another nest.

Forty-eight days into the operation, the watchers on this and all the other nests suffered a 24-hour hiccup. On 4th June 1943, Conder noted: "Owing to the escape of some officers and the ensuing checking up of same I was unable to watch birds." An ingeniously cut tunnel had led 67 men out of captivity. Buxton informed Marjorie: "A very successful escape (67 of us) took place the other day and has had the usual result of a peevish exhibition of bad temper – you shan't have any more music, or theatre or games and so on." For all their ingenuity, within two weeks all 67 were caught and on their way to Colditz Castle.

After nearly three years behind barbed wire, Conder had been through all that and had no further interest in cloak-and-dagger escapology. His enthusiasm for his chosen birds was waning too. Three days after the escape, he cast envious eyes upwards: "After the rain this evening 2 pairs of House Martins were investigating the southern wall of the abort between block 1 and 2. There were circling over the football field and then flying up to the wall. I was not able to look at it for very long as I was watching goldfinches." Other birds tempted him and disturbed his sleep: "An icterine warbler was singing well at 03.50 this morning. I looked at the watch then went to sleep, but I think it had awoken me. Later at a more reasonable hour of c06.30 it was still singing."

By the end of that week, he had embarked on a supplementary project, which he wrote up when he knew he would be leaving the camp:

Bird feeding heights Eichstätt June 11th – 27th 1943.
These are the very thin results of the slight investigation I made into the heights at which birds fed. Notes were taken principally when I was watching Goldfinches in front of block 1. The notes were taken during a fortnight from June 11th to 27th and are not an accurate result so can only be taken as a guide. Further investigations which could have been continued if I had remained at Eichstätt might have shown a difference in heights across a period of months, especially in birds that feed in trees.

As it was, the results for sixteen species were spectacularly underwhelming: "Blackbird – on ground. Yellowhammer – mostly on ground by dustbin. Great tit 15" in sycamore. 11" in lime (average). Moorhen – on surface." And so on.

The Buxton-led redstart study that had begun with such a song of promise ended with a month of anticlimax. The poor exhausted female completed her fourth nest; the confused male sang at more than one nest. The female abandoned the nest; the male sang less. The men concluded that "the birds' sexuality had declined" and sure enough, first the female and then the male disappeared for good.

Yet if it was a failure, it was a glorious failure of massive proportions:

I was able to gather together a mass of notes on one pair covering eight hundred and fifty hours in the months of April, May and June 1943. No pair of birds have ever been watched so continuously, with their every movement recorded, and this could not have been done, even in prison, without the willing and conscientious help of many of my fellows... some of our most delightful hours in those years were spent, pencil in hand, watching the bewildering actions of those two redstarts.

The birdwatchers were galvanised by their work. An excited Buxton told Marjorie that they had "studies by GW, JHB, self and another [surely Peter Conder]. We have got so much that is new, by working in a way never done before – as I did in 1941, and we could make a valuable book I think."

Maurice Waterhouse, who had a hand in the redstarts' fate in more ways than one, had shared the euphoria. In an immediate post-war letter to Buxton he wrote:

> I found myself constantly back in "C area" where we wrote, thought or talked Redstarts Redstarts Redstarts – And how fascinating it was! And how varied! There were cold spells and wet spells, half-hours solitary and half-hours social; it could be uncomfortably hot or just right; there might be time to talk to the passing Simon Green, or no time for anything but concentrated writing at GFR's* dictation. I shall never forget the Wryneck assault when there was no

---

* George Raeburn.

hope of recording everything, yet I felt obliged to down pencil & stone Wryneck. In case I've not done so already, let me thank you for having introduced me to all this. It was time most profitably and enjoyably spent.

Conder continued with his labour as before. In a letter home on 20th June, he complained: "I am still watching this wretched Goldfinch and I find it stupendously boring sometimes. Something inside says I have got to go on. So I do." But one week later, he knew that his own watch was coming to an end. On 29th June, he informed his father:

Moved again is the cry. As I write this I have not left the camp yet but am all ready to get going. So far I don't know my destination but no doubt I'll soon be told. Half of my old room are going. I cannot say it was the best half because there was no best half. We all got on tremendously well, even though when we were first thrown together we hardly knew each other by sight. The first secret was, I think, to take absolutely nothing seriously, the second was that everyone liked quiet. I also leave behind 2 chaps, by name Bertie Evers and Vincent Hollom, with whom I have been for the last three years. That is rather a pity, but it can't be helped. The loss of the birds and my fellow bird-watchers is another blow. I have learnt much from them, but I could learn a lot more. Luckily the last Goldfinch is just finishing, and I have got most of the stuff to work on during next winter. I shall probably have a brain-storm by the end of it. I am taking things rather philosophically, which is all you can do, and all I've got the energy to do.

* * *

On his last day at Eichstätt, Conder was unable to watch over his second nest, for he was locked up and searched in preparation for departure. But other watchers stepped into the void. That evening, at one minute to eight, it was John Buxton who closed the watch with "End. No further movement". On 1st July, Bertie Evers noted: "The two chicks finally left the nest at 0615." Peter Conder left Eichstätt on the same day. Three gold-finch nests were still active when he departed. Nobody watched them after he'd gone.

Waterston's wryneck nestwatch was like no other: he berated his observers on a daily basis:

> Please write legibly... Please write only in the blank spaces... Please conserve space in your notes... Before passing on your notes to the next observer, please re-read and see that they "make sense"!... Please sign your initials and give time when you took over etc... Please keep a close watch on the box hole as on three occasions the bird entered or left the hole without being noticed... Two cases of faulty reading today.

His demands could be exacting: "Would observers please try and find out where the adult birds collect food (ie in their spare time)... Would observers please try and collect faeces for examination."

Nor were all of his methods universally approved. A wayward genius for improvisation had Waterston constructing a "home or away" indicator to detect whether the birds were in the box.

He pinned a weighted piece of thread over the hole that would be pushed in or out by the entering and departing birds and then found he had to make adjustments to weigh it down still further. John Buxton was unimpressed: "I think new indicator is putting them off. If so, their eggs may be chilled." Waterston stood firm: "New indicator seems to work satisfactorily," he declared on the same day.

The master kept all his pupils obedient: three months after the watch began, it ended with the same thirteen men in Waterston's team. Maimie Nethersole-Thompson, a good friend in post-war years, recalled that the often blunt, sometimes hectoring tone in his writing was at odds with a modest, charming man, prized for his direct honesty. And perhaps the one aspect of his character that kept his assistants loyal and motivated was his infectious passion and care for the birds. He wrote that he "nearly fell off the ladder with surprise" when he opened the lid of the first nestbox to find five eggs inside, and there is a heartfelt sadness in his entry recording the nest's failure, almost at the point of hatching:

18 June 1900 Birds have not been at nest for over 5 hours. A bad day – has almost certainly deserted I am afraid GW

20.15 GW off to parade.

19 June 0700 Indicator caught up in wire and 3 broken eggs on ground (1 below tree and 2 on path to N of tree about 6 feet from box). All eggs contained well developed embryos and would have hatched within a week I feel sure.

0900 Took nest down. It contained 6 unbroken eggs all of
which contained embryos

And so Waterston carried along his gang of helpers. A brusque
instruction to record food being taken into the box met with a
willing response: "I had a good view of Wk's beak but could not
detect any scoff." There may have been some reward in being
told that at 3 hours and 19 minutes, the birds had broken their
record for a single period of incubation. They would certainly
have welcomed the rare praise: "Congratulations to all observers
on completion of today's observation without a single wrong
observation being made!"

Not all of George Waterston's assistants were given a pencil
or recognition for their watching endeavours. More than one
German guard stopped to assist, although with limited knowledge of the vocabulary of birdwatching, they would have been
of little practical use and perhaps stood in mute curiosity or
with an uncertain desire to help. Nothing was ever written
down and their names and efforts remained unacknowledged.
They were, after all, the enemy.

The whole wryneck watch combined high drama and low
farce. When the first nest failed in mid-June, the men switched
to a second, already filled with nine eggs. The incubating birds
were sensitive to disturbance. The birdwatchers stood aghast in
helpless contemplation as hordes of POWs were "rushing up
and down after some bees which had swarmed in the upper
branches" and noted that the timid birds were "even disturbed
by bugle blowing for Appel". Waterston tried to keep in his
men a sense of proportion: "It is unnecessary to specify in
minute detail the movements of the birds when frightened by

"One bird has been described as being paler than the other. If you can distinguish the two birds please record in your notes Wp for pale bird and Wd for dark one." – Waterston's watchers faced great difficulties in recording wrynecks.

passers-by", but then lost it further down the same page: "Please record carefully when birds are scared by passers-by. During the popular promenade periods in the evening, the number of visits [to the nest by the birds] is greatly reduced."

When four chicks of the second nest fledged on 24th July, the men had completed roughly 1,200 hours of observation. It was a staggering, perhaps unprecedented feat of dedication, but what did it amount to in its contribution to science? Absolutely nothing. George Waterston never found time to write it all up. Or rather, he never made time, realising that there were not so much gaps in the study as yawning chasms. These were amateur birdwatchers and, for the most part, lacking the patience, perseverance and skill of a Conder, they made amateurish observations. And they found that with the wryneck they had bitten off more than they could chew. One bird was light and one was dark. Some observers couldn't tell which was which. They concluded that the dark bird was the female, then changed their minds a week later. They distinguished the birds by spotting that one had tail feathers missing, then discovered that the other had tail feathers missing too. In the end, perhaps it was kind of Waterston to hold back the results rather than submit them to an ornithological journal and suffer almost certain rejection.

* * *

There was no such thing as downtime for George Waterston. When he wasn't watching birds, he was scheming in the barracks. An Edinburgh lawyer and ardent wildfowler called Ian Pitman, who "escaped" from camp routine by writing a slight book about shooting ducks and geese in Scotland, remembered: "You had to concentrate on something that interested you and take it for granted that you had a future. With one man it was designing a new type of tattie-howking machine, with George it was Fair Isle." Pitman would later play a major role in realising Waterston's dreams by securing a loan from a wealthy backer to buy the island. But for now, he and Waterston discussed at length possibilities for Fair Isle. On the evening Waterston's wrynecks evicted Buxton's redstarts for the second time, he sat down to write a final draft of his proposals for the island and his own pivotal role in its future. This was Waterston's business case, right down to the calculation that a half-capacity hostel would register a directors' profit of £355 4s. Waterston drew an artistic impression of his beloved Pund cottage, complete with an extension, and included a perfectly executed floor plan. There was just one little snag. Waterston shared his aspirations and sought advice in letters to the island naturalist George Stout, who wrote back in the summer of 1943 to say: "With regard to the house at Pund, I really can do nothing meantime, owing to occupancy and alterations, but cannot give details." What Stout could not disclose was that the army had taken over the island and, by accident or design, had managed to burn down the cottage.

THE BARRACK ROOM WRITERS

The absolute must-read in Eichstätt was the camp magazine. It was called *The Magazine* and perhaps it was named with more than a touch of irony. There was but one copy. Writers handwrote their contributions and artists pasted in their work. There was no such thing as distribution of this monthly journal: "*The Magazine* may be seen upon application to Malcolm Fry, Block III, Room 3."

It captured the interests and showed the great learning of a select number of talented prisoners. The coinage of Edward the Third rubbed alongside the music of Bach, the latter piece penned by redstart watcher Maurice Waterhouse. Other camp naturalists were regular correspondents. Surprise surprise, Buxton featured in every issue. A number of his poems gained their first readers in these camp-bound volumes.

Swifts

See there, the brown, mad swifts
Scything the wide swathes of air

Blades which are bright aglint
With the sunlight's use and wear

Listen! how they screech and scream
As they whirl round the prison walls,
Till speed flings them suddenly beyond
Like wine-drops spun from bowls

Oh! these brown, mad swifts spinning round
In play or after tiny prey!
O my spirit, where are your wings?
Spread them, bear me away.

Buxton dabbled effortlessly in other fields, producing features about Welsh and Norwegian poetry, as well as writing an obituary for the ornithologist Harry Witherby. The news was hardly current – he had died four months before.

Another regular was zoologist Richard Purchon. He became one of the most popular men in camp when he discovered a colony of edible snails within the grounds and sought to capitalise in print on the cooking opportunities such a discovery created. In "Escargots" by RD Purchon, he extolled – tongue in cheek – the virtues of this select and tiny dish: "In this matter of original recipes, let us get away from those Beetonian excesses which parade under the name of 'an economical hot pot for eight'!" Purchon recommended fasting and then boiling the unfortunate molluscs:

Serve hot, with or without a piquant sauce according to taste. About 6 snails per person makes a satisfactory savoury. As an alternative, one may slice the boiled snails and fry with a batter of german* mustard (best quality) Klim** [dried milk], grated cheese and margarine, and serve hot on toast.

Why not try snail farming and market your fattened four year olds in the dry season? The habit is growing! Get snail minded.

Purchon also answered one of the great unmusical mysteries of the summer of 1943:

When I was first asked what it was that made the monotonous "crie crie crie" notes in the grass banks, I was unable to give an answer. This was intolerable, for I was accosted daily on the subject and the mysterious notes which hammered the brain throughout the day pervaded the night also – one was given no rest.

Search for the hidden singer drew blank until one day when I saw a dark brown form bolt into a small burrow. A few minutes' excavation were rewarded by the capture of an insect which was indubitably an adult mole cricket.

Purchon would eventually "rescue" a number of the crickets and keep them in tins to observe his captives' behaviour, as well as return to the grass banks to watch their wild cousins.

George Waterston made his camp debut with a prose-lytising piece on the observatory on the Isle of May. He followed up

---

* A quite deliberate and probably derogatory lower-case g.
**Tins of milk powder. The Nestlé tradename spelt milk backwards.

with an article that conveyed something of his feelings about captivity.

"The Biter Bit!"
Some years ago, I had occasion to visit a Zoo, and being principally interested in birds, I made my way to the Aviary.

Perched on a guano-spattered tree stump in a dark corner of one of the cages sat a Buzzard, with wings hanging loosely and head sunk low on its shoulders, utterly dispirited and with lack-lustre and disinterested eyes it watched the milling throng of gaping humans swarming before it. A piece of raw meat lay in the sawdust in another corner.

"Poor bird," I muttered softly, "it really is damnable."

As though she heard and understood what I said, the bird raised her head slightly, and seemed to regard me for a moment with a gleam of interest, before relapsing once more into her normal state of coma.

My last recollection was of a dull shapeless mass of brown feathers – a mere travesty of one of those glorious free creatures which used to delight the eye in the Western Highlands.

+ +

A few years later, I was walking round the compound of a Prisoners of War camp in Germany, gazing with envious feelings at the little dabchicks as they dived and swam in the sluggish river which meandered through the pasture land outside the barbed wire.

Suddenly a Buzzard came soaring over the brow of the hill, swept out over the valley, and planed slowly round in ever-widening circles in the blue void. Flexing its wings it changed course, sweeping downwards in powerful gliding bounds – moving effortlessly against the breeze. I got a splendid view of it as it slipped past at close quarters, its keen eyes searching the ground near the river.

I watched it until it disappeared over the spruce-clad hills to the south; and then I continued quietly on my way, my mind filled with strange emotions.

+ +

I could have sworn that bird winked mischievously at me as it winged onwards – free as the air in which it moved!

Every article in *The Magazine* was copied out without a correction or a blemish, and for a very good reason. The publication had a particularly exclusive readership and prisoners were keen to see their efforts sent out into the wider world as well, if nothing else, to remind it that they still existed. Every article was honed and neatly finalised before it was copied in.

Waterston posted hand-duplicated copies of the articles to Bruce Stenhouse, the son of his old professor friend, perhaps unaware that correspondence sent to Edinburgh might not reach his "literary agent", who was otherwise occupied with the Royal Artillery in North Africa and Italy. Waterston gave clear instructions about where "The Biter Bit" should be published:

Send to:- The Editor "Bird Notes & News"* 82 Victoria Street London SW1 with explanatory details of what we are doing in bird-watching here – erection of 26 nesting boxes – 65 species seen to date – John Buxton etc etc. Afraid my subscription to the Royal Society for the Protection of Birds has lapsed due to War.

Waterston could not have known that wartime paper shortages at home had reduced the RSPB magazine to just sixteen pages. His article was never published.

* * *

Two of the most brilliant contributions to *The Magazine** came from unlikely sources. An Ellon solicitor called George Raeburn, one of the redstart watchers of '43, was inspired by his summer vigil to pen a piece of comic genius.

BIRD-WATCHING MADE DIFFICULT

The glowing popularity of bird-watching is such, that unless the weather-beaten veterans of the profession are to be crowded out of all the most desirable stances it is imperative that a small practical manual on the subject be published for the guidance and discouragement of the keen young observer. Pending such publication I would venture to point out some of the difficulties.

The more obvious snags require no elaboration. Among them may be classed weather, wire and crickets, black spots in front of the eyes, fog, foliage, cats and wrynecks.

---

* At that time the title of the RSPB magazine.

The amateur bird watcher has however to contend with numerous more subtle and perhaps more dangerous enemies particularly as regards that branch of the profession which may be termed "Identification and appreciation of species" and it is the purpose of this article briefly to expose some of the pitfalls for the unwary. The order in which they are set forth is in no way significant but merely the outcome of prolonged concentration and a disproportionate attention to birds. They are:-

All Fellow POWs Especially Friends. The observer will frequently find on taking up a favourite stance, that he rapidly becomes the centre of a swarm of his fellow beings. This is embarrassing but not so embarrassing as the next development, which is the question "What are you looking at?" For the answer must generally be "Nothing." And this is not calculated to impress the audience. While should the observer by any remote chance be studying some rare bird, admission of this fact will cause him to be sharply elbowed aside and possibly trampled underfoot. Accordingly he is advised either to complete his bird watching early in the day before the general public is on the move or speedily to acquire the reputation of a licensed bird watcher. This is best achieved by presenting a keen bespeckled appearance eg wearing a kilt, a beard, red hair or a faraway look, although a combination of all these distinguishing features should be avoided as being considered a trifle outré even in modern bird watch circles.

The Pundits, the Olympians of ornithology who are apt to pour from the Parnassus of their knowledge douches of exceptionally cold water upon the more imaginative discoveries of the keen young observer. At the same time, unless of a very rude or very evasive disposition, he will find himself smoothly incorporated by them in the recording staff – an aspect of bird watching outwith the scope of this article.

The Female Yellowhammer is a very sinister foe. It is a common bird. It is unlike its husband. Its plumage varies with the seasons. It resembles many other rarer species. Thus it is one of the trump cards held by the Pundits, and the aspiring observer will find it a hard task, in his early days, to identify any bird, other than a crow, which might not equally well be a female yellowhammer. This becomes rather monstrous.

Bats and Aircraft sometimes resemble birds, particularly if the observer is myopic and deaf.

All Hawks are a twofold trial, as in the first place they are prone to remove and eat the bird which is being watched, and further they do this so suddenly, so speedily and at such improbable moments that they afford the observer no opportunity of diagnosing correctly to which species the aggressor belongs. He is advised therefore to divide all hawks into (a) buzzards, b) unidentified predators, except on windy days when buzzards too should be included in this category (b).

Pseudo Nightingales. The observer will soon find that many normal brother officers hear nightingales singing by night while he does not. This admission will involve him in a grave loss of prestige and it is of little avail to talk glibly about the possibility of reed warblers or owls being the true sources of the midnight music, as his own infallibility on the subject of nightingales is the honest belief and proud boast of every Briton, and many Dominion officers too.

Bad Potatoes. The nocturnal peregrinations and subsequent sessions induced by these result in a great increase of pseudo nightingales. Consequently they are very hostile.

Bees and Butterflies. The former may threaten the observer by direct action or hordes of eager apiarists in pursuit of conglomerations of bees may intimidate a valuable bird. Butterflies are not a direct menace, but they are generally closely followed by John Lainé* who is.

The Starling, the Icterine Warbler and the Marsh Warbler. These birds are all noted mimics. That is to say, they sing one another's songs instead of their own. So the observer can seldom be sure whether he is listening to an icterine warbler mocking a starling ragging a marsh warbler or vice versa, which is very confusing.

The Waterhole by the South East corner of the football pitch is a self-evident snag but should be borne in mind particularly in moments of excitement.

Snoring. The keen young observer will probably read in the text books that barn owls, tawny owls and little owls make a snoring noise. This should not cause him to forget his own bitterly acquired knowledge that this despicable practice is not confined to owls.

---

* One of the two officers appointed as camp butterfly and moth recorders.

The Golden Oriole is a snare and a delusion. It has not arrived which is sad because it is really rather a lovely bird.

Frogs are absent. This may seem irrelevant, but is not. Had they been present, any indeterminate avian sounds might successfully have been passed off as emanating from them. Accordingly they must (in their absence) be considered hostile.

The Sexual Appetite of Sparrows is so gross as to offend the gently nurtured observer. It may on the other hand arouse in him feelings of envy incompatible with that scientific detachment of mind with which such phenomena should properly be viewed.

The Kingfisher, the Yellow Wagtail and the Black Kite. These species should be treated with contempt. They are arrant snobs revealing themselves only to the Pundits.

Long Parades. These are a menace because during them the more sensitive birds are apt to feel neglected and peevish, through not being watched.

The Ball Game and the Bagpipes. When either of these national pastimes breaks out all right-minded birds take to the woods. In certain perverse birds, however, they evidently arouse an unfortunate spirit of emulation. Thus the woeful wail of the wryneck rises above the strains of the pibroch, and the war cries of the base ballers are drowned by the fearsome rasping croaks of the angry great reed warbler. Which is all very horrible.

The Chiff Chaff and the Willow Warbler are virtually indistinguishable in appearance and so present a dangerous trap. The sole clues are that in the former the legs are always black, while in the latter the blackness of the legs varies in proportion to the cleanliness or otherwise of the trees which are its habitat. In any event the legs may only be seen with the aid of powerful field glasses at the range of 6 inches and further both species are indistinguishable from the wood warbler.

Finally All Textbooks are hostile. The bad ones are misleading and the good ones support the Pundits (see above).

It is to be hoped that by now the keen young observer has lost something of his fervour. Further he must realise that the above list of enemies is by no means exhaustive. Should, however, he still remain unshaken and determined to proceed with bird watching he may eventually be included in the ranks of accredited licensed bird watchers. This may appear to him to be a desirable thing but let him not be deceived as to what it means. He will become the butt of his friends, an eccentric pariah to the main street, an object of suspicion to the sentries, the plaything of the elements, the prey of all manner of insects and a pain in the neck to his P.M.C. [President of the Mess Committee]

But he fondly thinks "I shall be admitted to the noble brotherhood of bird lovers, and that is compensation indeed." Which is a grave misapprehension. For the Pundits will cynically set him on a stool, notebook in hand, the meanest serf of science. The near Pundits will snub him. And the rank and file will jealously set out to blast and wither the budding reputation of a possible rival. They will glibly (and incontrovertibly) convert his nutcrackers to starlings, his twites to female yellowhammers and his ospreys to unidentifiable predators. This talk will be to him a meaningless jargon – all of acrocephalines and accipitridae, scapulars and undertail coverts. They will quote freely and nonchalantly from Witherby and Niethammer, Heinroth and Linnaeus. They will exchange obscure quips about whiskered terns and dusky tits. In short they will do all they can to make him feel a complete outsider.

He must then surely see that it were far better for him to revert to normal healthy pursuits. His interests once more will centre on poker, the football league, and the parcel

*"SKYLARK (*Alauda arvensis*) Resident and breeding throughout the area, also a few passage migrants. Scarce in winter so probably some migration away from the district. Song began 20.2.43, 15.3.44." John Buxton*

situation, and he will be able happily to say – with our gallant ally "I guess a boid is just a boid to me."

Buxton's fellow librarian ANL "Tim" Munby generally spent his spare time writing ghost stories, but on one of his rare ventures into *The Magazine*, he captured the wry amusement with which other prisoners viewed the birdwatchers:

The Song of the Wryneck

Though the box is labour-saving
It necessitates the waiving
Of the right to any privacy of life:
All this peeping and this prying
Is particularly trying
To a sensitive and newly-married wife.

When your mind is set on mating
It is quite exasperating
To see an ornithologist below:
Though it may be nature study
To a bird it's merely bloody
Awful manners. Can't he see that he's "de trop"?

How would Waterston or Purchon
Like a bird to do research on
The way in which they propagate their clan?
Thank the Lord! The bugle's calling
And they'll have to go and fall in
Now for twenty minutes love-life while we can!

pent his spare time writing short stories, but one of his rare

BOAT TO THE ISLES

Aug 19th 1943
I gave the last bird talk last Sun., but, though GW seems
to take no interest, I have two excellent "pupils" and really
we've done a lot.

In his letter to Marjorie, John Buxton was clearly delighted
with two unidentified protégés, but what had happened to the
second lieutenant? Buxton was showing an unwitting lack of
consideration, for by the end of that summer, a kidney stone
was causing George Waterston increasing bouts of excruciating
pain. The uncomplaining Scot had been taken to the camp
hospital earlier in the year. Thorough investigations followed,
but when the German medical officer told Waterston that
nothing could be done for him, Waterston replied in a flash:
"There is a surgeon in Edinburgh who can put me right. His
name is Henry Wade." Much to Waterston's astonishment, the
medical officer replied: "You are quite right. I know of Henry
Wade."

In that moment, Waterston's passage home was all but
secured. He had passed the repatriation board on 16th May. Yet

still there was a long wait – the exchange of prisoners no longer fit for active service had been pursued successfully since the Great War and was enshrined in the Geneva Convention. But the German authorities, with hundreds of thousands of POWs in their hands, were laggards at implementing swaps as long as the Allies held only a few thousand of their own men. In that summer of 1943, the bargaining balance shifted. Thousands of Wehrmacht soldiers were being captured in Africa and at last the German authorities were willing to trade.

Potential repatriates had to go through a rigorous vetting procedure involving examinations by three medical officers. The lionised and now visibly ailing General Fortune, who had led Peter Conder's 51st Highland Division in Normandy, was offered the chance to go home but declined, saying: "I got my men into this mess. I'm going to lead them out of it." George Waterston would later regale friends and colleagues with the story of how his own birdwatcher companion Ian Pitman decided to try his luck: "So, Captain Pitman, why do you think you should be repatriated?" asked the stern German official sitting behind his desk. "Because I've only got one eye," answered Pitman, reaching up to his face, pulling out his glass eye and placing it on the officer's blotting pad.

A letter reached George Waterston in Barrack 3 on 29th September. It was from his longstanding Fair Isle friend (and very irregular correspondent) George "Fieldy" Stout. The old man signed off with: "I am keeping in good health and trust you are also in the best and bucked up by the turn of the tide." Just five days later, John Buxton had lost his friend from the barracks. He told Marjorie: "This has been a great day for

George W (and others) have left for home!… I hope GW will get well soon. I know he'll write to you. I hope you can see him. He is one of the (very few) people I shall want to see afterwards."

Ill though he was, Waterston had important things to carry. There were his letters, diaries, the precious battered notebook he had carried around Crete, his proposals for the future of Fair Isle and the records from his wryneck observations. There was also an article mapping out a future for bird observatories, which he had co-authored with Buxton and which would appear the following February in *Country Life*, illustrated with pictures of Skokholm taken by Buxton's brother-in-law, Ronald Lockley.

Fully laden, Waterston was put on a train and eventually arrived at Gothenburg in neutral Sweden, where 5,000 wounded soldiers waited to be evacuated. He walked on board a Red Cross boat, bound for the Edinburgh port of Leith. In a rare act of orchestrated neutrality, a Nazi destroyer accompanied them into the North Sea, and a Royal Navy vessel met them halfway. But rather than steering directly into the Channel, the ship headed round the far north of Scotland to avoid mines. Waterston was brought up on deck by a sailor's cry: "I think the most emotional moment of my life was when somebody shouted 'Land ahead' and there, only two or three miles off, was the Sheep Rock at Fair Isle standing out in the sunshine. The tears ran down my cheeks – I knew it so well, and it had been so often in my thoughts."

Waterston did not fall under the surgeon's scalpel until the following year: "I underwent my first operation on 14th Feb. A large stone about the size of a pigeon's egg was removed from my left kidney… I have been given sick leave until 24th April when I have to return for my final operation to the other kidney."

Waterston's idea of sick leave was rather different from most patients'. In the recuperative gap between operations, he raced off to go birdwatching on Orkney, then cadged a lift in an air-sea rescue launch – to where else but Fair Isle?

off to go birdwatching on Our ney they dodged a lift in an

BIRD BROTHERS

While Buxton, Conder and Waterston enjoyed the best part of a year together in the pretty valley of Eichstätt, John Barrett was rather less fortunate in his surroundings. Only days after he left Warburg in September 1942, Barrett nearly lost his life inside a cattle truck. The train that carried the RAF contingent pulled into the sidings at Posen station in Poland on the night of 5th September 1942 and narrowly missed being hit as Allied planes launched a bombing attack.

In the morning, the men were taken on a short journey and through the gates of Oflag XXI at Schubin. Barrett was housed with his fellow RAF officers, but now he found himself the only birdwatcher in the camp. He gained the name that stayed with him for the rest of his captivity – "Birdie". (Peter Conder was given the same name – it seemed to attach readily to these lone birdwatchers). The new arrival noticed the great stick nest that a pair of storks had made earlier that year on the hospital roof. Someone told him that the ornamented eaves of the building, once the mansion house of the estate owner, had held nesting house and tree sparrows that summer. But right now, the autumn migration was bringing a big passage of birds of prey. Soaring high, almost out of sight, their identity was not debated as it would have been at Warburg. Barrett mused alone.

He quickly found solitary pleasure from early-morning walks around the perimeter fence, well before the hubbub of the masses drove away the birds. There were woods beyond the boundary and, on the other side of a road, a marsh. As Barrett fell into a routine, so too did the camp security officer, a man he judged to be in his late fifties. The officer habitually greeted him in English with a "Good morning, old sport. And what have we on offer today?" The conversations were necessarily brief, for anything longer would have aroused suspicion, but over the next few weeks, the two men found common ground. Here was a man who had once sold books to the fathers of the men he now guarded. The German officer had graduated from Oxford, and had been sent to fight in the Second Battle of Ypres – the same battle in which Barrett's own father had been killed. He had gone back to Oxford after the Great War to work in a bookshop, learning the trade, before returning to Germany to open one of his own.

Barrett saw an opening in the discussions about books, for now he had none. The precious illuminating volumes of Niethammer's *Deutsche Vogelkunde* had remained with John Buxton. Barrett explained that his attempts to obtain copies through official channels had come to naught. The officer expressed sympathy and shrugged.

Some time afterwards, a guard came into Barrett's hut carrying a brown-paper parcel and asked: "Herr Major Barrett?" "Yes", replied the curious officer. "*Für sie!*" said the soldier, who placed the parcel on the table and promptly swivelled and marched out of the room. Barrett unwrapped the unlabelled package to find the complete three volumes of *Deutsche Vogelkunde* inside.

He disclosed nothing to the others in his room about the books' likely origin. He said nothing to the camp security officer the next day, but looking him in the eye, thought he saw a slight nod of the head. Barrett was never able to thank his kind benefactor. Perhaps someone had seen too much. At any rate, he never saw the German officer again.

The Polish winter was particularly hard on men who slept in huts one brick thick. Ice formed a lining three inches deep and Barrett shivered in his bunk, covered in a horse blanket,

Barrett watched birds of prey, storks and cranes (pictured here) alone in the autumn of 1942.

and fully clothed with three extra pairs of socks, a balaclava and thick mittens. During milder days, he set to work writing up the huge numbers of notes on tree sparrows that he and Purchon had made in Warburg the previous summer.

Spring had barely begun when the RAF boys were on the move again. Stalag Luft III at Sagan would become notorious as the location for the famous Wooden Horse escape and the most famous escape of all – the Great Escape itself. Sagan was a dreary, clear-felled patch in the middle of a pine forest, the huts thrown up on bare, sandy ground, raised on pillars to deter tunnelling. The camp was subdivided into compounds. Barrett's men in the east compound were completely shut off from their fellow RAF officers in the north compound by an eight-foot fence.

Just before they left for Sagan, Barrett had acquired a bird-watching partner. They were now two out of 1,700 men. Flight Lieutenant Alfred James Barnard Thompson (known variously as Barney or Tommo), POW Number 203, was 24 years old and had arrived in Schubin in March 1943: "I asked the camp adjutant (a pompous character) if there were any other POWs interested in birds. 'Oh yes. Squadron Leader Barrett, hut K, extraordinary fellow, says the sparrows here are not ordinary sparrows.' 'Hooray,' thought I, for I had already noticed that they were tree sparrows and I knew that he must therefore be a reputable ornithologist."

Less than five weeks before, the young RAF officer had had his one and only taste of aerial combat. On his first mission – a raid on the U-boat base city of Lorient in Brittany. Barney Thompson's Wellington bomber dropped its load and the ground was lit up with explosions. As was standard practice,

*Each prisoner was given a POW number. To the Germans,
Barney Thompson was Gefangennummer 203.*

one of the crew took advantage of the temporary illumination
below by taking a photograph for future reconnaissance. The
camera flash sparked, the camera burst into flames and within
seconds, the plane was a fireball. Barney Thompson baled out:
his four crewmates all perished.

Barney was given temporary shelter by a French peasant,
who gave him clothes and put him on a train bound for Spain.
He spoke no French, and fellow passengers guessed the mute
passenger's identity. A nun fed him a hard-boiled egg. At
Bayonne, just twenty miles short of the border, German security officers boarded the train... and that was that.

Barney had been shot down on 4th February, and, for
two months, his family in Gloucester were left in a limbo of

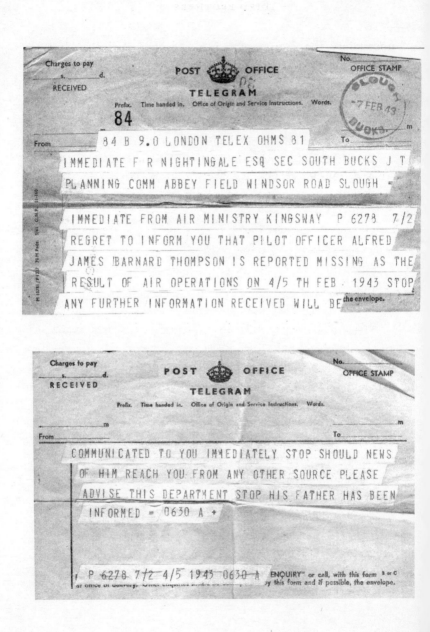

Charges to pay s. d.
RECEIVED

No.
OFFICE STAMP

POST OFFICE

TELEGRAM

Prefix. Time handed in. Office of Origin and Service Instructions. Words.

84

From

84 B 9.0 LONDON TELEX OHMS 81   To

IMMEDIATE F R NIGHTINGALE ESQ SEC SOUTH BUCKS J T
PLANNING COMM ABBEY FIELD WINDSOR ROAD SLOUGH =

IMMEDIATE FROM AIR MINISTRY KINGSWAY P 6278   7/2
REGRET TO INFORM YOU THAT PILOT OFFICER ALFRED
JAMES BARNARD THOMPSON IS REPORTED MISSING AS THE
RESULT OF AIR OPERATIONS ON 4/5 TH FEB 1943 STOP
ANY FURTHER INFORMATION RECEIVED WILL BE the envelope.

Charges to pay s. d.
RECEIVED

No.
OFFICE STAMP

POST OFFICE

TELEGRAM

Prefix. Time handed in. Office of Origin and Service Instructions. Words.

m   m
From   To

COMMUNICATED TO YOU IMMEDIATELY STOP SHOULD NEWS
OF HIM REACH YOU FROM ANY OTHER SOURCE PLEASE
ADVISE THIS DEPARTMENT STOP HIS FATHER HAS BEEN
INFORMED = 0630 A +

P 6278 7/2 4/5 1943 0630 A   ENQUIRY" or call, with this form ᴮ ᵒʳ ᶜ
ᵃᵗ ᵒᶠᶠⁱᶜᵉ ᵒᶠ ᵈᵉˡⁱᵛᵉʳʸ. ...   by this form and if possible, the envelope.

uncertainty. The planning office in Slough, where he had worked as a draughtsman, received a telegram on 7th February:

IMMEDIATE FROM AIR MINISTRY KINGSWAY P6278 7/2 REGRET TO INFORM YOU THAT PILOT OFFICER ALFRED JAMES BARNARD THOMPSON IS REPORTED MISSING AS THE RESULT OF AIR OPERATIONS 4/5th FEB 1943 STOP ANY FURTHER INFORMATION RECEIVED WILL BE COMMUNICATED TO YOU IMMEDIATELY STOP SHOULD NEWS OF HIM REACH YOU FROM ANY OTHER SOURCE PLEASE ADVISE THIS DEPARTMENT STOP HIS FATHER HAS BEEN INFORMED

News of Barney's internment eventually reached home, and his brother wrote to the Red Cross in Geneva, hoping his message would reach his imprisoned sibling:

13 Bearland, Gloucester
5th April 1943 [*"received 31st May 56 days" – Barney
noted on the letter*]

Dear Old Boy

We were all tremendously relieved to get your first letter a day or so ago and find that you are safe and sound. Mum and Dad were terribly worried until the good news came through, but they have cheered up now and are merry and bright once again. We are writing to you c/o the Red Cross in Geneva until such time as we get a permanent address, this may mean a delay before you receive mail but is the best we can do for the moment. We have had enquiries from lots of people about you.

Hope you are still managing to do a bit of Bird watching. I will try and get some bird books sent out to you when you settle down. A card arrived from the British Trust for Ornithology recently to tell you that the black headed gull you found dead on the River Severn was ringed when a nestling near Copenhagen about a year previously. I did want to send you "British Birds" but as it is a periodical I don't think it will be allowed. As it is a scientific work it may be permissible but I shall have to get further information about it.

The summer migrants have started to arrive and there are chiffchaffs singing from most of the woods now. I have been out for several rides on the bicycle with a pal I have been working with, and am getting him interested in birds. Your kit won't be released until you authorize it in a letter or a card to us. So perhaps you could do that; we do know that everything is intact though. We have carried out your request about the photograph.

Keep smiling my boy

Peter

Throughout his life, Barney Thompson had been remarkably close to his younger brother Peter. As teenagers, they had cycled the lanes of Gloucestershire together looking for birds. Birds (and trains) still bound the two young men together. At the outbreak of war, Barney signed up for the RAF. He was sent for flight training to South Africa, where he quickly learned about the Allied censor's scissors. Whole passages were neatly snipped from letters home. But his bird notes were left uncut. The lesson stood both brothers in good stead for their prolific correspondence to and from captivity.

Barney arrived at Sagan in mid-April and sent his brother three postcards in four days. He noted in the first: "The last camp showed great promise but we left just as the first chiffchaff arrived."

The second postcard provided a torrent of observations:

> In this camp we hear redstart, willow warblers, black redstart, greenfinches, chaffinches, siskins or serins, yellowhammers, wood larks, crested larks, mistle thrush, coal tits, crested tits, cuckoo and ringdove. On passage we have had wheatear, hoopoe! Red kite, swallow, chiffchaff, tree pipit, storks and linnet. No sparrows here at all and no thrushes or blackbirds yet. Don't expect to see much variety here after spring migration.

Peter knew his brother had been captured when he wrote to him on 12th April:

> I must keep up the good work and write to you regularly in the hope that you will eventually get some of these letters. I am trying to organise some bird books for you but can't do much until I get your permanent address. I still manage to do a bit of birdwatching – the latest arrivals are willow warblers which are now singing well and telling us that spring is here.

By mid-May, Peter still had no direct word from his brother. His letter of 16th May would provide a poignant reminder of home:

> There are corn buntings singing away outside my window at this moment, greenfinches and linnets and larks are also singing near at hand, and a pair of oystercatchers are chasing each other across the meadow with shrill pipings. The latest arrivals of the summer migrants are the swifts – I noticed the first ones two days ago though this is really a bit late for them. My list of migrants is very patchy and incomplete this year as I have not had much time out bird-watching lately.

A week later, Peter wrote again:

> 24th May
>
> I haven't had much leisure for birdwatching, but occasion-ally see birds on my way to work. I had two new summer migrants back in the week – sedge warblers which were singing heartily from round a small lake and sand martins which are nesting in the banks of the river. Both of these are very late but have probably been here a long time before I noticed them. Yesterday I was watching swallows picking up mud and straw from the farmyard puddles for their nests in the barns.

Eight hundred miles away, his brother was seeing a different and much later spring, cramming a seven-line postcard with nothing but bird observations:

28th May

Have been seeing a lot of jackdaws recently feeding on a
field near the camp, a jay almost daily – looking for nests
and causing much excitement to chaffinches and others…
a flock of martins once and Barrett has seen buzzards.

He did manage to squeeze in at the end "Hope you have
been able to get a few days out."

A few days later, the prisoner had reason for celebration:

2nd June

I received your first letter a couple of days ago and
was immediately cheered to read it. I had not expected
anything for a long while yet so it was doubly welcome.
I was glad to hear that my black headed gull had been
traced OK. Thanks for your efforts re sending out
books but I don't think British Birds will be allowed –
at least Barrett says not and he is an old prisoner and
should know. I really don't know what books I require
for Barrett is well established and has all the German
handbooks, which he translates for my benefit, & a
couple of English ones – one of the condensed Cowards
and a Wardlaw Ramsay, so we are really quite well off.
We are keeping systematic daily records of the camp,
which prove very interesting. Our daily list is very small
but select – usually about 20 but includes crested tit,
crested lark, black redstart and so on. Today has been a
red letter day and we added five new species – lapwing,
black headed gull (both passing over at night), golden
oriole a long hoped for bird which we heard all day and

saw twice, & common and lesser whitethroat, so you can see that things are rather late here. We have also seen crossbills on a number of occasions recently, storks often and a kite yesterday, whilst we have definitely identified serin at last.

Thanks a million for the letter and best wishes to you and the folks

Cheeriho, yours, Barney

Peter to Barney:

2nd June

I am glad to hear that you have found someone else interested in birds. Do you require any bird books? Let me know if you do and it may be possible to get them sent to you.

I am writing this in my bedroom – the window is open and there is quite a chorus of evening song. Blackbirds, willow warblers, greenfinches and wrens are making the main contributions, but there are also blue tits, linnets and a distant but persistent cuckoo to be heard. The cuckoo is the last summer migrant to be added to my list – I heard him first about a week ago – this is disgracefully late but I haven't been out a lot this summer.

Peter to Barney:

14th June

I have been interested in your bird notes and am glad to find you are still adding to the lists. I have passed through some very fine country lately but haven't had the time to investigate it unfortunately. Lately I have been working at night and nearly every morning hear a fine dawn chorus of song as I come home. This morning was a red letter day as I heard a corncrake calling from a field of crops. I haven't all my notes handy but I think this is the first record of the corncrake for three years.

I didn't get up till lunchtime today and then was able to spend most of the afternoon sleeping in the garden. Most of the birds are busy feeding their young now but there is still quite a lot of song. We have lots of greenfinches, linnets and chaffinches and the odd pair of yellowhammers and willow warblers piping up. This probably sounds idyllic to you but I am really working quite hard, and am hoping to have a short holiday soon.

An uninformed reader (such as a German censor) would have scanned this letter and concluded that Peter Thompson was employed in some kind of night shift work and passed over it. In reality, the afternoons were spent sleeping off a night in the skies, for Peter was an RAF bomber pilot, taking part in raids over Germany.

Barney to Peter:

23rd June
A new sp for the camp – a grey wagtail recently. Yoiks! Letter just arrived dated May 16th and one from mum. Much joy!

Barney to Peter:

7th July

Thanks for all the news and notes – it is good to hear of the birds you have been seeing & I could visualise the places you visited to see redstart and sandpiper when you were out near home. I envy you oyster catchers and things too, but no doubt you envy me the storks & orioles – though we do not see much of these jokers.

Peter to Barney:

[written while on leave – or "holiday" as he was always careful to describe it] 15th July

I have been out on the bicycle several days revisiting our old haunts but things are pretty quiet just now. Song has dwindled to a minimum and it is the young families that are most in evidence – young chaffinches, parties of tits, rows of whitethroats waiting to be fed by parents and so on... I have been taking Dad along with me on some of these rides and he struggles along in the rear. He says that his legs aren't as young as they used to be, but the real trouble is that he tries to climb all the hills in top gear!

Barney to Peter:

17th July

Was very pleased to receive another letter from you today, dated 30th June. Nothing much to write about from here so here goes for some bird news. S/Ldr Barrett and I are keeping joint notes of the camp's birds and write up our summary of notes each fortnight and make up also a sheet of bird numbers like my sheets of the sewage farm. Last month was our best so far, which was a surprise. Of birds of prey, we saw Buzzard, Kestrel, Hobby, Kite and Sparrow Hawk – all definite and not queries as usual. Of course, a mere list makes it sound very attractive here but we only get occasional glimpses of such things. Feeding, actually in the barbed wire, we see young willow warblers, black redstarts and commons (less often) gt & blue tits, pied & spotted flycatchers (on odd days), & white wags & crested larks – an interesting combination.

Barney also noted that the pair had heard first-brood chaffinches singing – "an interesting discovery of ours this". Undoubtedly, Barrett's daily vigil on a chaffinch nest the previous summer had made him extra alert to chaffinches' every move and sound. Barney rounded off his letter with a little knowing line that spoke coded volumes: "Best of luck, my boy, now that you are really down to business."

Peter to Barney:

24th July

I discovered that the red-backed shrikes are still nesting near Churchdown. On three occasions I saw them in Badgeworth Lane and saw the old birds feeding the fledgelings. I suspect that there were two pairs breeding, but can't be certain.

Peter Thompson's records that summer provide a mid-twentieth century snapshot of bird life in south-west England.

His brother would have expected to hear reports of red-backed shrikes and corncrakes. The former was a sporadic breeder by 1943: both would be extinct in England by the end of the century.

Peter to Barney:

31st July

I am now hard at work again and have almost forgotten my holiday. The bird life now is still quite interesting – the willow warblers seem to have resumed their morning song and it is very pleasant to hear them piping away from the woods as I walk along the road before breakfast. There are turtle doves here too and this morning they were purring away in the distance. That sound immediately brought to mind our walks across the Surrey commons – in the hot summer sun with the drowsy crooning of the turtle doves and the old grasshopper warbler "reeling" away intermittently. Well, mustn't go on in that strain or you'll be getting homesick. I had a stroke of luck today – on my way to work I have to cross a potato field and coming back this evening I put up a wheatear from quite close to the path – unfortunately he bobbled away over the hedge... but it is a sign of the times, I suppose. The return migration has just about started.

Barney to Peter:

7th August

Glad to hear you have been visiting some of the good old spots and how I wish I could have been with you.

Unfortunately the censor had been at work on your letter and what looks like an interesting sentence is quite blacked out, confound it. [The offending sentence reads: "Yes I find you are right ████████████ there is some ████████████████ and it can't be ████████████". The obliterations are made with black sealing wax.] Have seen a buzzard here for several days now and a cat caught a wood warbler in the camp – our only record of one as yet.

Peter to Barney:

23rd August

Dear Old Boy

I haven't heard from you since last writing but must give you a further account of my doings. The main item to report is a new species added to my list. This is a woodcock which I saw about a week or so ago. It was almost dark and I was walking up the road between the woods and the woodcock came sailing over – he looked like a big moth with quick, irregular wing beats and as he went overhead I saw his head and long bill looking down. Naturally, this was a red letter day for me and it cheered me up no end.

Barney to Peter:

23rd August

Almost unbelievable – a fieldfare today but they breed in Germany so it is not so surprising really. Hope you are doing well these days – I'm envying you like anything.

Barney to Peter:

27th August

This month has been exceedingly interesting. Things had dropped right off – young birds were hatched, no song & most of the birds seemed to have moved to the fields; then we had a passage, mainly to the south-west which still continues and almost anything might turn up. Tawny pipit is the greatest triumph so far – we have probably overlooked them before, but lack of glasses is a considerable handicap. Blue-headed wags & tree pipits have been trickling through for several days, a wheatear has appeared near camp and shrikes & both flycatchers have been through.

Barney to Peter:

10th September

Many thanks for your letter of 31st July, received a few days ago. As usual, the only news of interest from this end is of birds. I was interested to hear of your wheatear late in July. Our first one here was third week in August & it looks as if main passage is in first half of this month as we have had several passing through lately... The later migrants are just beginning to come through now – meadow pipits, chaffinches, an odd hooded crow, yellowhammers, the first skylark today, unidentified small finches and very confusing movements of swallows and the first martins seen yet in big numbers. Of night we have heard curlew, dunlin, cranes & unidentifiables.

Barney to Peter:

28th September

Well, the first tang of autumn is in the air now & the birds have been keeping us busy counting them as they go over so here goes for another description. Swallows – we saw big parties on roosting movements through last half of Aug and first week of this month with several probable days of migration. Skylarks appear daily and are suffering from "pre-migration unrest" & mill around in all directions... Hawfinches showed up on a roosting movement, one goldfinch went over (our first here), as yet only one redwing – a dead one found in camp – but 3 fieldfares and many song thrushes on migration at night.

In his notebook, Barney drew four buzzard wings showing the main patterns of plumage he and Barrett had seen. The illustrations bore more than a passing resemblance to aircraft wings.

Barney to Peter:

25th October

Mail here has been very poor lately and I haven't had any letters from home for over 3 weeks... Much has happened in the bird world here since I last wrote... Song thrushes we heard passing in big numbers every night for about a week & on one night a few ringed plover, so our list of waders is imposing now, though our only records are of odd calls like this heard in the night.

Barney to Peter:

19th November

We are really down to the blank winter days. It is quite surprising to find all our familiar birds like chaffinch, robin, thrush and so on as completely migratory as swallows and chiffchaffs at home. You can guess how much we will be looking forward to the spring. My mail has been very poor recently – I have only had three letters in the last 7 weeks and none of them from you or from home. Could you send on a copy of the Oxford Bird Report please? Barrett here knows Tucker* well, so we'd both be glad to see it. Hope things are going well with you – I'm rather anxiously awaiting news now. All the best. Cheerioh, Yours Barney

Barney to Peter:

27th November

Not seeing much these days. Main thing is an evening roosting movement of Corvidae – mostly Hooded Crows & Jackdaws & each day we see crested larks and great tits in camp. These are the only regulars now & the stragglers are great sp woodpecker & other species of tits. Saw two buzzards one day & once a white wagtail – these left ages ago. Surprised at lack of redwings & fieldfares here this month. Hope you are keeping OK. Anxious to hear from you.

   Yours Barney

---

* Bernard Tucker – lecturer in zoology at Oxford, editor of British Birds.

Barney did eventually receive the Oxford Bird Report that he had asked his brother to send. A month after the war's end, he wrote to Bernard Tucker, and the Oxford lecturer generously despatched copies covering Barney's missing years, adding in a covering letter: "The last I heard of you was when your brother wrote to me in 1943 to say that your plane had been shot down over Germany and it was feared that you had lost your life... I am indeed delighted to hear that you are safely back."

Barney's brother Peter was not so fortunate: on the night of 22nd September, his Halifax bomber was shot down during a raid on Hannover. Peter Thompson stayed at the controls of his plane long enough for most of his crew to bale out safely, but he was unable to save himself.

* * *

All through that summer and autumn while the Thompson brothers had exchanged letters, the prisoners at Sagan were engaged in a subterfuge of memorable cunning. The accommodation huts were raised two feet off the ground on brick pillars, rendering digging beneath impossible. But outside, a little way short of the wire, two officers had set up a vaulting horse for gymnastics.

Just about every day for four months, the home-made wooden horse was carried to the same spot and every day a man hidden inside would drop to the ground, remove a concealed cover and dig a little more of the tunnel while prisoners vaulted over the horse under the eyes of the guards. John Barrett was one of the vaulters, but he was also given the role of organiser, making sure there were enough vaulters to fill the session, fixing up who should remove the excavated sand and where they would dump it.

Barney Thompson was posted on "Goon watch", checking both birds and guards. On evenings in his hut, he would put his skills as a draughtsman to use in drawing maps for the escapees. On the evening of 28th October, the three diggers surfaced on the other side of the wire with Barney's maps in their possession. All three made it back to England.

That winter, Barrett read voraciously and took up chess in a big way. He and Thompson also ensured that they spent at least four hours every day – either singly or together – birdwatching. They seemed to gain vicarious delight from little birds going out of bounds – a small group of tree sparrows on the wire sheltered under a sentry box from the rain, another: "had a narrow escape from a sparrowhawk – it dashed into the barbed wire in the nick of time". And the men delighted in the innocent audacity of some great tits: "5 March – A female investigated one of the sentry boxes… Pair seen investigating NW sentry box on several occasions. One on 31st was seeking food within 3ft of the sentry's head."

They used their bird notes to poke fun at their captors. The men tired of the daily loudspeaker announcements blared out throughout the camp fabricating German victories and playing military marches. Criticism took a variety of forms:

Note re chirrup calls in general

Does a musical note if given sufficiently loud jar upon our ears to give a "chirrup" effect? Wireless loudspeakers at full blare are "woolly" and certainly jar one's ears!

Memories of Warburg must have flooded back to John Barrett towards the end of March, as another great crow migration took place. His junior companion collected old dental record cards for the occasion. One stated that a Sgt Neil received treatment on 1/12/42 and 3/12/42. The backs of these dental cards were put to a new use: Barney filled them with notes as more than16,000 "Rooks & Jacks" passed overhead in less than a fortnight.

The two birdwatchers kept their sanity… while others lost theirs. Surrounded on all sides by dark conifer forest, Sagan was especially oppressive to men who were now enduring their third or fourth year of captivity. The guards tormented their prisoners with the word "Katyn", a Russian forest where more than 20,000 Polish POW officers had been shot in 1940. The guards were implying that one day they might deal out the same fate to the Allied POWs.

In the north compound over the fence, the Great Escape, the best-known POW act of the war, took place without any of the men in Barrett's compound having the slightest inkling of anything happening. They were told on the parade ground that 52 men had been "shot attempting to escape". One prisoner asked how many of those had been wounded. The German officer said nothing. The message was spelled out in those words – from now on, anyone found outside the wire was a dead man. The utter hopelessness was too much for a number of prisoners: in the following months they simply ran into the wire and died in hails of machine-gun fire.

Spring brought promise… and another year without fulfil-ment. It was a great disappointment for Barrett and Thompson that, in two years, not a single bird bred within Sagan. There were a few tantalising "if only" observations:

The patriotic crested lark. The prisoners heard the bird's song as "God Save the Queen".

Mistle thrush
Only definite proof of breeding was that a bird was seen carrying food in bill & making regular trips across camp 20-26 May 1944.

Other birds – wheatears, common redstarts and many more – came and went, merely passing through.

One species, however, was resident, and occupied huge amounts of the birdwatchers' time. Crested larks, they concluded, were possibly what they called the most static species in the area, recorded on more days than any other. The birds hunted among the cabbage and potato crops in the prisoners' vegetable garden, took seeds from under the trip wire and perched against the warm chimney bricks on cold days. Yet they did not nest within 100 yards of the wire, and Barrett later said: "It was tantalising to live so close to a new species for so long and have no chance to learn more than its song, calls and shape." They observed:

> Birds are at all times very indifferent to humans & allow approach to within a few yards with no sign of alarm. Usually on approach they merely run to one side, only flying if one is too persistent or careless…
>
> The following foods were seen to be consumed
> Leatherjackets, caterpillars, millet, corn spurrey seed…
> Small amount of Reich bread 30 Nov '43
> Scraps of food in garden – Dec '43

The bread and scraps were only eaten in bad weather when little else was available, and were not touched at other periods of the year, when sparrows fed on them. Barrett was always quick to praise other people's superior skills. He soon came to value Thompson's exceptional ear for song and calls: "Our first description in April '43: 'Song has continuity of skylark and quality of woodlark, but is not quite so mellow, being more "silvery" in quality.' In the absence of recording equipment and sonographs, Thompson constructed elaborate song charts. The written word of transcription could not keep up: "We have a note of 'see eep' calls 26-29 Feb '44 but I think this is an error. We had not then differentiated between 'seeeep' & 'see ooo' and all calls thro' Mar. & April were 'seeooo'."

The distinctions between less musical species were beyond the human ear. Under jackdaws, Thompson commented: "Assessment of 'song' has proved difficult, so many notes used which might mean different things – calls, song, alarm, conversation, anger – sounding alike to me (have decided that song chart for this species is valueless)." He heard a lot of jackdaws that autumn, for they came on their return migration in greater numbers than they had seen before. On 25th October, the peak day of passage, they counted 23,500 jackdaws and rooks.

Some of the excitement of those days of migration even touched one of Thompson's otherwise uninterested messmates. Pilot Officer Richard "Dick" Winn, 450 Squadron Royal Australian Air Force remembered:

In camp one day, Tommo rushed into our room very excited "The migration of the... tit has started." The rest of the inmates scoffed at him – I was interested and asked him to show me. We went outside to one point on the circuit with a view over the cleared area of the surrounding pine forest. I expected something big but could not see anything – very disappointed and I said so. Tommo said "Look over there – there goes one." "That's not much of a migration," I said. However about every five seconds another tit would fly across – going in the same direction – south. I still was not impressed. Tommo said this is going on over the whole of Europe – we are seeing here one bird every five seconds over an area of 75 metres – this means when all are added together there are just millions heading south to North Africa. All this taught me a very important lesson – we go through life missing a great deal.

It's hard to guess what bird Dick Winn was looking at.

At the onset of winter, Red Cross parcels all but stopped and the men began once more to experience gnawing hunger. Men and birds alike resorted to opportunistic improvisation. Under hooded crow, the *Nebelkrähe*, which Barrett translated as mist or fog crow, the men noted: "On Dec 12 1944 one seen to carry a small tin several yards in its feet. It then pecked at it for some time and finally flew off with it in its bill, dropping it like a gull dropping shellfish. Performance repeated twice." Less salubrious was the observation that "Heaps of stable manure usually attracted hoodies – particularly when ground frozen – & freshly sprayed human excreta never failed to bring in a party of c.20 who fed eagerly on the stuff, or possibly the maggots it may contain." One particular individual caught their attention: "Bird with right foot missing seen almost daily. It seemed to hold its own at first but once ground was frozen it was at a disadvantage being unable to hammer frozen food, as do the others, without overbalancing. It fled away from the crowd and was chivvied by other crows & even rooks. Of necessity, it fed closer to the wire and later each day than the other birds." Another prisoner confessed many years later that out of desperation he had caught, killed and eaten a "one-legged crow". Did Barrett and Thompson find out? And did the prisoner know just what that bird had been eating?

On the penultimate day of 1944, a crested lark was dead in the camp. Nobody knew how long the bird had been dead or if its body ended up in the stew. But one thing was certain. Barney carefully detached the wings and tail and wrapped them in a copy of the Nazi newspaper, the *Völkischer Beobachter*. He wasn't intending to give them up in a hurry.

Barney's crested lark wing, still wrapped in the original German newspaper. Note the word "Kampf", meaning battle or fight. References in articles to "Dezember" and a story about the American advance date it to either the end of December 1944 or very early in January 1945. Barney left Sagan on 27th January.

OUT OF EDEN

No sooner had George Waterston been packed off home than the Eichstätt gates opened a little bit to let a very select band of twenty men out on weekly parole walks through the town, into the woods and down the valley for two or three blissful miles in either direction.

So-called parole walks took place in many POW camps from the summer of 1943 onwards. The whole notion was quite bizarre. The contemporary Oxford English Dictionary defined parole as "the undertaking given by a prisoner of war that he will not try to escape, or that, if liberated, he will return to custody under stated conditions, or will refrain from taking up arms against his captors for a stated period". It was in the prisoners' collective interest to honour the promise, for to break it would have denied the privilege to the whole camp. Certainly, in spite of the very high ratio of prisoners to guards, none attempted an escape on the regular walks that were to follow, even when opportunities were handed to them.

For Buxton, "this was a delight beyond realisation except by men who have been confined within barbed wire for years. To walk for some distance in one direction, to wander about in woods or across fields – what joy it was after our walks had only been up and down, up and down, or round and round close to the curtain of wire, with every movement overlooked by the sentries in their towers, our every footstep placed where some other prisoner had a few minutes before placed his and where another would soon follow."

The Eichstätt prisoners' known horizons expanded, and so too did the camp noticeboard. Early in September, John Buxton had begun posting up a weekly news bulletin of natural history sightings which prisoners were asked to report to the relevant recorders by 9 o'clock every Sunday morning. Buxton (birds), Purchon (mammals) and others covering insects and flowers would collate the findings and Buxton would type them out on sheets that were stuck on the canteen noticeboard that evening.

Those first walks brought birds never or rarely seen by the prisoners before. The woods yielded goldcrests, nuthatches, long-tailed tits, treecreepers – everyday species for birdwatchers who had the ability to walk where they wanted, but a treat for men denied such delights for more than three long years.

Much to Buxton's dismay, on occasions the weekly walk turned into an expedition to the cinema in town. Half the camp went along in November, under strict instructions from the senior british officer not to boo the Nazi chiefs. Buxton went too, although he would have cheerfully swapped a film about the Strauss family for a commune with nature. But the big screen did have its compensations: "I went this am – a good break in this dreary monastic life even to see pictures of a girl – that now scarcely credible creature."

Other walks, as autumn turned to winter, became so-called "stumping parties", wood-gathering sorties to fuel the prisoners'

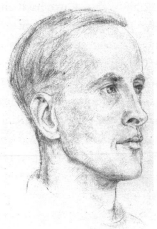

*John Buxton, sketched by a fellow prisoner and sent to
Marjorie Buxton on St Valentine's Day, 1943.*

stoves, as always under armed escort. One day, parole walkers
found a starved rook in town that was so weak the prisoners
were able to catch it and take it back to camp. The men fed and
restored it to good health before releasing it two days later. One
record posted on the canteen noticeboard that week made for
interesting reading:

Mammal
Common shrew. 2 found dead on 4th.
The Rook ate one.

The weekly bulletin of sightings broadened, and not just in
terms of birds. Purchon, the appointed mammal recorder, made a

special plea: "Notes on birds etc. seen on parole walks are welcome; and it would be especially interesting to have notes on abundance of voles in various areas. If possible the number of holes in a square yard should be counted. Voles seem to be very abundant in the valley but less so in the hills." An amateur astronomer supplied monthly star updates and pencil drawings of constellations.

One little discovery of local import provided an interesting titbit: "It may be of interest that ARCHAEOPTERYX LITHOGRAPHICA* was discovered in a quarry to the west of the Schloss. This is the most primitive bird known – the earliest creature known to have possessed feathers and to be adapted to use them for flight."

* * *

At the end of the flying season, Buxton posted up a list of butterflies that had been pinned up on boards by the camp lepidopterist. For once, Buxton was typing beyond his own knowledge. A tally of skippers was preceded in the list by a "Lulworth Slipper" and the error was compounded by a "Small Slipper". Even Buxton nods.

Though the noticeboard showed an active interest in natural history among prisoners, it was a niche market. That autumn and winter, Allied troops pressed up towards Rome, the German army was pushed back in Russia and American forces cleared the Japanese invaders from atolls and islands in the Pacific, one

---

* The farmer who found this, the most complete specimen, sold it in 1876 for the price of a cow.

by one. For the men of Eichstätt, the end was in sight and many of them intensified efforts to build for their future. Prisoners sat exams in subjects such as business and accountancy, invigilated by officers under strict exam conditions and marked by examiners back home. Richard Purchon, the one professional naturalist, taught lessons for a degree in zoology, an initiative set up by the Red Cross and London University; solicitor Bertie Evers offered courses in law.

A South African captain called Dearlove devised a questionnaire that was completed by 300 officers. He found that, on average, officers spent two and a half hours a day engaged in study. One hour and sixteen minutes were whiled away in "aimless gossip". "Hobbies" occupied just six minutes a day. The officer concluded: "Naturally there is very little scope for this form of activity. Popular are bird-watching, butterfly-collecting, collecting various brands of cigarettes, coins (?), razor blades; designing homes, motor-cars, yachts."

Buxton began 1944 with plans for the breeding season ahead. He wrote to Dr Stresemann in Berlin requesting a substantial number of bird rings. It was a big ask in wartime, especially as, in January alone, more than 3,200 bombers targeted the German capital, killing thousands and rendering hundreds of thousands homeless. Yet clearly Buxton's plea reached a willing and able recipient. On 20th February, he told Marjorie: "Better things were the receipt of rings and coloured rings from ES (tell George)." Ever careful, Buxton always called Stresemann only by his initials in his letters home. It wouldn't have done for his benefactor's full identity to have been spotted by the censor.

Now suitably equipped, Buxton posted an announcement in the bulletin:

Note on ringing

A number of rings have been received and it is to be hoped
to be possible to construct a small trap so that adult birds,
and not only nestlings, may be ringed. Any birds caught
in rooms etc. should be brought to J. Buxton III/12. In
the Spring, information about the site of nests (especially
those found on walks) will be welcome.

Sure enough, the men made four little cage traps and set them
out; one sat on the parade ground, another on the outside of
the football field. A male chaffinch was their first captive, dropping in on 24th March. Throughout that spring and summer,
Buxton caught and placed little coloured rings on more than

*"WHITE WAGTAIL (*Motacilla alba*) Summer resident and
breeding throughout the area. In 1943 3 pairs bred in or about
the camp, in 1944 2 pairs." John Buxton*

60 birds – chaffinches, greenfinches, great tits and numerous swallows in the camp. On parole walks he ringed chicks in the nest – red-backed shrikes and yellowhammers. Of course, nothing would come of all this effort – the prisoners would not be there to see through another spring and in the war-shattered continental Europe of 1945, there were probably few who had the means or inclination to catch the ringed birds and record their movements.

At the beginning of migration, encouragement came from an unexpected quarter. A German non-commissioned officer had some interest in birds and flowers, and a willingness to provide for his prisoners. He took parties out on very early-morning parole walks to hear the dawn chorus. Buxton's gratitude was bittersweet: "This was the bewildering contrariness of the Germans' treatment of us: one day they would take a few of us on a walk to hear the dawn chorus; the next day they would take away our bedding."

* * *

The men that Buxton had trained were now more experienced. Buxton noted: "In 1943 only two of us were able to identify such birds as great reed warbler, icterine warbler, black kite, green sandpiper, in 1944 ten or twelve could do so." In those days before field guides, identification of tricky species, especially without binoculars, was extremely difficult. That year, the birdwatchers found two "new" species in camp that had been there all along. The short-toed treecreeper, "of whose field characteristics we had no reliable description until Spring 1944", and grey-headed woodpecker, a dusky variant of the green woodpecker, were positively identified. And of course, the men had problems with gulls: "It should be noted that we had many records of birds identifiable as gulls or even as "large gulls" or "small gulls" which are here omitted owing to uncertainty in identification." Buxton entered into some debate with Stresemann over his herring gulls, which the German ornithologist suggested might have been lesser black-backed gulls. The British ornithologists kept to their guns by insisting that at least two of the birds they had seen were indeed herring gulls.

Buxton kept up a regular correspondence with his repatriated friend. There was surely a coded message about the forthcoming D-Day landings in a letter that Waterston wrote in late March 1944: "There has been a small waxwing invasion this autumn... Look out for big war news in the near future." Why would Waterston throw in a note about the appearance of waxwings in spring when the event had happened months before? The word "invasion" placed close to "big war news" cannot be a coincidence.

Buxton was in a positive frame of mind when he wrote to Marjorie on 11th April: "I celebrated (too early!) our 5th anniversary with the best day thru 4 years – a lovely sunny day with white clouds and I was out for a walk for over 3 hours outside this damned wire. Jacko Macleod and I walked together, and both agreed it was our best day in prison – we found a wonderful place for birds, with our sweet willow-wren singing – do you remember? Chaffinch, song and mistle thrushes, blackbirds, dunnock, many robins, green woodpeckers calling, nuthatches, great, coal, crested and marsh tits, goldcrests, larks and many more and best of all a nightingale jug-jugging, and the 1st cuckoo of the year… So many people notice nothing but to me the country is always so teeming full of living things, I am quite breathless trying to keep track of them."

There were to be no sustained nestwatches for Buxton that year. Redstarts came fleetingly – time enough for one to be ringed – but none stayed in the camp to nest. Not that Buxton was greatly bothered, for he had already told Marjorie: "The redstart is back and singing, but I shan't spend so much time on it this year, as I can't add much to what I already have."

A spell in hospital with chicken pox gave Buxton a psychological health check:

> The doctor who looked after me in prison read my poems and said I'd kept a very balanced outlook in spite of so long in prison. In fact I have to thank you first, and then my ability to enjoy the moment with birds and things, because my roots are so deep in simple things and passionate things no war can ever touch. It is the townies who go mad but there is none of us free from strain.

Purchon's swallows returned that summer, with interest. The camp buildings thronged with swooping birds. Nineteen pairs nested, eleven of them producing second broods. Purchon and his team kept an irregular watch "due to administrative difficulties" to produce rigorously scientific findings. Purchon pondered in the camp magazine:

> We may well pause here to consider what useful purpose has been served by expressing the percentage incubation

as a cubic regression. We cannot assert that such a formula expresses a fundamental rhythm in the vital processes of the bird for the sequences in the incubation period might be independent. The best fit might be a parabola intersected by a downward sloping straight line, the point of intersection at the 8th or 9th day representing an abrupt change from one type of equilibrium to another.

Exactly. Buxton was as puzzled as anybody by Purchon's mathematical cogitations, writing: "This is Purchon's stuff that I laboriously calculated but I don't know what it's about even now."

Purchon struck a more popular note when he discovered a new colony of edible snails outside the camp. There was a huge rush of applications to go on the following week's parole walk. Even the bunk potatoes stirred themselves to apply.

Moths and butterflies proved a great attraction that summer, thanks mainly to an improvised breeding cage. Men were invited to inspect the caterpillars of such as the garden tiger, elephant hawk moth and puss moth. Outside that little box of captive wrigglers (situated between the hospital and the quartermaster's stores), the camp was a collector's dream, with no fewer than 24 species of butterfly on the wing daily during one week in August. A perfect specimen of a Camberwell beauty was caught in a cigarette tin. The officer reporting the find preserved class distinctions by not bothering to ascertain the collector's first name. He was credited on the noticeboard only as "Private Relf".

That summer, George Raeburn had watched over a red-backed shrike nest which produced four young. When the birds had flown, he turned his attention to the swallow roosts that in September were building up among the reedbeds on the river. The second broods left the camp in the middle of the month, coinciding with a peak number of 1,200 swallows dropping into their night roost. Raeburn's team of watchers took their timings from the camp clock – in his words, "a notoriously fickle piece of mechanism".

That autumn saw John Buxton's mental reserves severely stretched. A psychologist who was also a POW observed that for prisoners: "the first year was spent in adaptation, the second was the best year, the third began to be a strain, and the fourth and following years left no one unscathed." As far back as 31st July, Buxton had written: "I'm busily trying to polish off my redstart stuff before coming home, which surely can't be long now." But Allied troops in faraway France were making slow headway and the wait for liberation seemed interminable: "We're all rather dreading our 5th winter especially with less fuel, less G rations... don't expect any poems – I've hardly written any all this year." Two of Buxton's companions cracked; one ran to the wire and began to climb. Another somehow persuaded the guards not to shoot. He in turn became agitated and Buxton walked him round and round the perimeter fence in an effort to calm him. The following day, the friend who had restrained the guards from shooting had lost all self-control. He was taken away to an asylum.

The men dutifully recorded the passage of crows that autumn. In the last month of the year, the camp bulletin featured an item of home news: "At the annual meeting of the British Trust for Ornithology Waterston (repatriated October 1943) gave an account of the breeding biology of the Wryneck, based on a study made here in 1943. He is also to broadcast a talk on Bird Watching from a Prison Camp." One of their number had found a life in the outside world. For the rest came their fifth Christmas in captivity.

On parole

The pendulum movement of Peter Conder's captivity had swung north again. Moved out of Eichstätt before the goldfinch nesting season was over, he walked through the gates of Oflag IX A/Z Rotenburg, in the central German state of Hesse, on 3rd July 1943. His initial impressions were unfavourable. His disappointment spilled over in the pages of his notebook: "After Oflag VIIB this camp is very bare. It is small and the trees are mostly chestnut with a birch and a few cherries. There is practically no grass, mostly asphalt, and a small vegetable patch." Writing home, his account concentrated on the old lags he discovered there:

> If there were fewer people in it, and a few more of rather a different type, and a little more exercise ground it might be quite reasonable. Some of the original inhabitants are pleased to see us because they say we might bring life into the camp, but I think the vast majority hate to see us for the same reason. How I wonder if "dead beats" would be the word. Some of them remind me of the story of the

man who sat in the same chair in his club night and day for a week.

At least one of Conder's birdwatching companions from Eichstätt stayed with him – Captain "Bobbie" Middlemas, a career soldier with the Royal Northumberland Fusiliers, who had taken a handful of later shifts in his goldfinch watches, as well as Ernest Edlmann, a messmate from his earlier years. Clearly there was at least some knowledge of birds among those who were already there: "As regards the birds nesting in the camp. I have been told the Goldfinches, White Wagtails, Spotted Flycatchers and Common and Black Redstarts here all produced first broods. The Black Redstarts had 2 nests both under the eaves of porches amongst the upright supporting beams. Now 3 pairs are nesting in the camp and again all 3 are in similar situations in the topmost attics of the buildings."

A letter for POW 346. The red stamp shows that letters from Britain were censored by the British as well as the German authorities.

The new camp brought fresh routines of irregular disturbance and new opportunities to add to the prisoner's bird list.
Difficulties of identification, known to all British birdwatchers
going abroad, were now his and his alone to solve:

I have finally decided that what I thought was a siskin is
now a serin. So many things were against it – the song
did not entirely agree with the handbook description,
for it is a very fast song that rises and falls in pitch for
c3 seconds. The song flight is very similar to that of the
Greenfinch, the wing being fully spread and beating
slowly. The song used in flight is a longer affair than
usual… I can write it down rather badly as "tirritir-
ritirri". They usually go about in pairs. When the
male lands and sings sometimes the wings are slightly
drooped. Sometimes as they fly past a yellow band
around the beak is visible.

Four days after his arrival came the first of many experiences
that would transform his time in captivity:

I think there is one good point about this place and that
is the parole walk. I went this morning with about 80
others and two Germans, along a track for about 2 miles
between the corn and along the river bank until we got to
a meadow where some people bathed. It was the first time
I've walked that distance without having to turn a corner
every 100 yards or so for 3 years. There was almost a faint
whiff of freedom about it.

By the time he had gone on his third two-hour walk beyond the camp he had re-learned something that he might have forgotten during more than three years of captivity: "Going out, I count every bird I see or hear taking as much care as possible not to count the same one twice." No longer was the sitting birdwatcher waiting for the birds to come to him – he could even go out to find them:

> When we are allowed to go on further than the bathe place it is possible to get quite close to a wood. Today a robin and a chiffchaff were the only birds singing from it. But I suppose the line of the ground and the canopy of the leaves have given to the song that peculiar resonance which I often found in the woods at home. In a prison camp one finds few opportunities to hear such a thing as this.

The "whiffs of freedom" that Conder described were indulgences that, at Rotenburg at least, appeared to be hidden from the ordinary German people. By the middle of 1943, none would have been spared hardship or the death of a loved one and they might have viewed kindnesses towards the enemy with a less than charitable eye. One civilian in the town said there was something clandestine about the walks. The almost furtive releases from the camp always headed towards the north-west, away from the houses. Many inhabitants ended the war unaware that they had even taken place.

Conder was doubly fortunate in the camp where he was now resident. Kommandant Bormann, a major in the Great War, was a committed Anglophile. He had been headmaster in the days before the school was converted into a prison camp. A man with an easy air of authority, he was an obvious choice to take control of the 600 men. He earned the admiration and respect of the prisoners – so much so that some British officers returned to visit him after the war was over.

Bormann ensured that his charges were given numerous opportunities to step out. Less than three weeks since he had entered the camp, Conder was writing home:

> The walks and the bathing make a tremendous difference and swimming is very good exercise. At the moment we are in the middle of a tremendous heat wave, in the sun it is unbearable, in the shade in a position where the wind can reach you it is too hot; in the room it is cooler but flies are a pest. (Evidently nothing can please me.) There are also some remarkable butterflies, Swallowtails and Tigermoths galore... There is only 1 bird that I have not seen before in Germany, a Black Woodpecker. While this heat lasts I can do nothing but laze. I read moderately tough books. Some time doing a little French or German. Both of which show some slight signs of improvement, but nothing I suppose to write home about. I can talk about birds quite well in German, but I start drowning as soon as any other subject crops up.

The morning walks were evidently both physical and psychological releases: "Only the parole walks make this joint alright," he said. Conder began bathing in the River Fulda, initially with some trepidation. In his weakened physical state, it proved a great exertion. And he had never been much of a

Conder was confined to the camp on the day he painted this
landscape of the view looking north.

The budding botanist picked 13 new species on his parole
walk of 3rd July 1944. He took them back to camp to identify
and painted this pretty pink.

sportsman. A colleague described him as "always rather slow in his movements. He much preferred sitting and watching". Yet he did stretch himself that month, dabbling in both hockey and cricket. And the enlightened *Kommandant* gave the officers the option of helping to build a prefabricated house nearby for a Swedish representative of the International Red Cross and the YMCA, whose home in Kassel had been bombed out. The men walked as slowly as possible to their building site destination, to eke out the amount of time spent beyond the barbed wire. While they were at work, Conder said he "never thought of anything but the present so that the camp was completely out of my mind".

All through July, Conder stretched his legs and his natural history knowledge. Another prisoner, John Cripps, was a keen botanist, so while birdwatching held him on the way out, Conder would tag along with Cripps on the return to camp, picking and drawing flowers as he went: "I picked three flowers to draw but I don't know what they were; one was a campanula of some sort, growing to about 3" in the bathe place." He was endearingly frank about his ignorance: "I have been intending to write a few notes on the willow for some days now but I find the subject rather difficult, because it is not a tree with which I have had much experience." Conder was a competent artist in watercolours, though his efforts were invariably accompanied by witty self-deprecation: "Downy woundwort – An awful picture, perhaps best to call it an impression but I don't think it gives much impression."

Another fellow officer had studied medical entomology before the war. It was a chance to go out and play with science, and an irresistible opportunity for Conder to play with punning:

*Conder's watercolours of flowers and insects seen on parole walks
in the summer of '44.*

I have been helping him recently in a study of burrowing bees. We have been trying some homing experiments over short distances, a mile to a mile and a half with some success. The first one had a fifty per cent success although it was the worst possible weather for the experiment. I had just released two more batches and judging by the way they went off the result will probably b* a success.

Though the afternoons back at camp proved hot and tedious, Conder found pleasure in his own company and achieved a goldfish-like delight in new discoveries as he went round and round his "bowl":

July 25th
In or about this camp three trees intrigue me and whenever I see them I have to look at them and wonder. The most important is the one I see most often when I lie out in the sun – the silver birch by the hospital... In a mood for contemplation, I look up at it for long periods. Walking round the square [just 200 square yards for 5–600 men] I watch it whilst I face it, or I may be reading beneath it, so that my eyes are caught by the careless movement whenever I raise them. The trailing twigs – not as long as at Eichstätt or Thorn – can seem like hair at times.

Attuned by three years of practice to the slightest of sounds, he was almost able to imagine himself somewhere

---

* Conder's little joke.

else as he heard a light wind in the branches. The writing is awkward, but the sense is clear: "I hear the ever-changing song, increasing, rustling, hissing, a deeper murmur from the branches. Sometimes rising so strongly that I can easily imagine a brook rushing over an uneven bed. The sound is soothing and cool."

Temperatures soared in August. On the first of the month, he wrote in his log: "These afternoons I find too hot outside. Inside, flies irritate me so much that I become annoyed and that is not conducive to the peacefulness I require for my well-being. So I am forced out of doors into the shade as far from noise as possible as there is but one spot – beneath the silver birch."

Conder sketched on every conceivable scrap of paper.

The stifling conditions in the overcrowded huts were not helped by the drawing down of blackout blinds at nightfall. Allied bombers had begun attacks on the city of Kassel less than 30 miles away in February of the previous year, but bombs also rained down on the railway marshalling yards of nearby Bebar. The people of Rotenburg prayed that the Allies knew of the prisoners' existence: perhaps they did; though one day an errant fighter aircraft strafed the camp and the prisoners emerged from their huts afterwards to feel the pock marks in the ground made by its machine-gun fire. Rotenburg itself remained bomb-free until two days after the camp finally emptied of prisoners. Only then did the first shells drop on the town.

On 3rd September, the fourth anniversary of the outbreak of war, Conder was wrestling with his conscience. For some time, he had been troubled by the thought that he should write up his work from Eichstätt. Now he confessed his self-doubts: "I hope to start some work on Goldfinches in a fortnight's time. I am looking forward to it, but with a great deal of fear. I have never attempted anything quite so big as this, and I have lost my two main advisers [undoubtedly he means Buxton and Waterston]." Meanwhile, a delicious wry humour was never far from the surface:

> By the way I've turned into a cricketer of no repute what-soever. It has the great merit of appearing to exercise you, whilst really doing nothing, not having to think about much, and absolutely no noise, rather a strange thing for this place. The captain has always won the toss, so we sit in the shade in the heat of the day, whilst the others almost

pass out. We straggle out after tea, and by our cool, smart fielding get them out before they know much.

Evenings were spent reading. A remarkably diverse range of books had begun to accumulate in the camp library, and very soon these started to exert an influence on the man with enormous amounts of time on his hands. Conder read *The Importance of Living* by the Chinese philosopher Lin Yutang and wrote in all seriousness: "Whether a pine is talkative depends on his physical state and his habitat." One book that had a distinctly practical effect on Conder's methods of study was *Watching Birds* by James Fisher. Back in July, he had been moved to write that it was worth its weight in gold and that he had read it time and time again. What did he make of statements in this 1940 popular classic such as: "There is only one moderately expensive tool which need stand in the way of anyone's evolution from a keen bird-watcher to a first-class ornithologist – this is a good pair of field glasses."?

On 20th September, he made a purposeful entry in his notebook: "I began a new method of counting birds which entails rather more work and difficulty but which will give fuller results. Every bird is put down under the type of ground on which I saw it." Fisher had given advice to take this approach in his "What you can do" chapter. Conder was perhaps less capable of following other admonitions such as "Make a trip to a sea cliff", "On your way to your place of holiday or on any journey, you can do transects" or "Join a national organisation".

The diversions and procrastinations to which Conder was prone continued all through that month, but by the 27th, he had at least taken a look at the work that he would have to do:

I am beginning to feel very shifty taking it moderately easy. But I hope that, if I've got sufficient in my old block to work it out correctly, the Goldfinch notes will be not entirely worthless. They will, I think, be certainly publishable in a scientific form, but the idea is that all the bird-watchers who have studied a species intensively should publish their results in book form which will probably be better for everyone concerned as the journals on birds would otherwise be swamped for several issues to come. As far as I can see it is going to take a very long time as I take an hour to analyse every hour that I watched, and sometimes it takes longer.

An appeal to home for paper with which to begin his task crossed in the post with two notebooks from Natalie: "Darling Sis. You're the cat's pyjamas. If I've ever said anything nasty about you, I'll take it all back."

On 20th October, Conder received news that boosted his sense of purpose. He had asked his family to contact Oxford ornithologist Harry Witherby, to ascertain whether any significant papers had been produced on the goldfinch. A negative response from the man with encyclopaedic knowledge brought some jubilation, for it meant that "what I produce is worth something". Conder had other news:

We've just got over a great excitement and are waiting to hear the result. All the people who were going to be repatriated left late on Sunday night, and it was reported or rumoured that they should be in Sweden or somewhere on the 19th. We were very sorry to see some of them go, but of course pleased for their sakes that they were off. Really it is surprising how little it affected the camp. Perhaps the uninitiated might think that an air of depression would settle over the place, but no – everybody's about the same as usual. After about three years or so you gain a tremendous sense of detachment and sometimes big things don't worry you. I am afraid I wonder if that phrase has the same significance at home as it does here. At any rate I have cultivated this sense of detachment very well, and having the endless study of birds to help, I get along very well.

The wounded and seriously ill prisoners, who manifestly could play no further part in any fighting, would join up with George Waterston in Sweden to be repatriated home. Meanwhile, big things were about to happen in the outside world. Two nights later, just 30 miles down the road, 569 British bombers dropped their loads on the city of Kassel. More than 10,000 people were killed and 150,000 rendered homeless in a firestorm that raged for seven days and nights. In the civilian wing of the camp, two sisters, who had already been evacuated from the city, stood and watched. They looked out towards the distant red glow of the burning city, then turned back towards the barracks when they heard loud cheering and saw prisoners on the first floor thrust their fists out of the windows in unison. The men carried on roaring their approval until gunfire from the guards silenced them.

The parole walks were stopped. It is not difficult to comprehend that this could have been an act of retaliation. Conder now buried himself in his work: "I spend all day now trying to write up my notes on Goldfinches, and I'm usually a mental wreck at the end of the day. I estimate that working at the same rate as I am at the moment I might possibly get it finished by the spring with luck."

Having been given almost four months of freedom on a leash, it was hard for him to come to terms with all-day captivity again, and a sense of weariness tainted his mid-November letter home:

It is a pity that there is no one to prepare you because naturally, I think that I have changed rather. I should have done. My method of life at the moment is of course adapted to the circumstances of the moment, and it would probably dishearten you, especially as it comes on top of another minor trial. But being a prisoner makes one mobile, not only in the goods and chattels sense, but also in habits and customs. Living all day and every day with 16 people of different habits might possibly lead to a rumpus. It is really surprising how little of this there is. I suppose everyone must practise a tremendous and practical form of self-denial. One of the first rules in a prison camp is to take nothing seriously, otherwise a gap is left into which the humorist cynics sail with great glee.

He signed off with rueful awareness of the length of time it took for mail to reach home and his life passing by: "Well, I suppose it's about time that I should wish you all a merry Christmas. It only seems about two months since the last."

Exactly one month after this gloomy note, parole walks resumed. The next morning: "A Blue Tit came to my bird table. It has a ring on its leg and is very tame allowing people to group at the window and look at it." Most likely, the bird had been ringed in the copse next to the camp that local people called the Vogelwäldchen – the little bird wood. The ringer was a teacher and avid birdwatcher who had now gone off to fight with the Wehrmacht. If only the two men could have met.

No sooner had the walks recommenced than the prisoners found what was most definitely a twitchable species:

A few yards up the river a duck appeared, a duck which caused consternation. We were on the river bank and the duck was in the centre of the river paddling downstream. It was about the size of a mallard, very dark or black all over. The beak looked dark grey. On the head were two white patches both just below the eye but one in front and one behind. It was swimming rather fast in the water. And did not fly although we were c.15 yards from it. The only thing that I can find which seems anything like it is a juvenile Velvet Scoter.

Christmas Eve had brought him the perfect present. Like an excited schoolboy, he noted: "Best view ever of the Velvet Scoter."

Bird news travelled, even in Germany during a war. Five weeks later, and several hundred miles away, John Buxton typed up his weekly nature bulletin at Eichstätt and concluded with the following item: "From Rotenburg – a Velvet Scoter is reported. It spent a fortnight on the river near the camp.

According to Niethammer this is the most frequently seen inland in Germany of the sea-ducks, though in Britain, it is very seldom seen inland." There was no direct contact between prisoners in the camps: was Berlin ornithologist Erwin Stresemann the conduit of this information? Nobody knows.

New Year's Day 1944 arrived with Conder feeling "moderately alright" and in a humorous vein:

Christmas began rather slowly, and worked up to a tremendous climax last night, followed by a day of moderate rest and feasting which is today. I am lying on my bed writing this in a most awkward position after lamb cutlets, peas and potatoes followed by Christmas pudding and brandy butter – the butter was alright but there wasn't much of the other.

In terms of natural history, he was scratching around. For 4th January his notebook entry stated: "On walk, JHC [John Cripps] and myself collected some mosses which we identified as fox-tail feather moss. It seems quite common but on the next walk we are going into its habitat here more intensively."

By February, he was beginning to catch up with the previous year's work, but perhaps without Buxton to chivvy him along, he was more inclined to be sidetracked:

Recently I have started my brain working at more than its accustomed rate. I think it is still rather startled. Part of this is caused by my finishing the end of the donkey-work of Goldfinches – the facts should all be easy to get at – so that I can start putting 2 and 2 together, hoping to make 4, but usually coming out at 1 or 5. But still it is rather more interesting. I have also started very gently reading some philosophy, which again keeps the old head jumping about a bit... After a winter that has been very mild so far, snow has fallen quite deeply, and already the ice rink is in action, and I hope that the ski run will be satisfactory by this afternoon. I constructed it on a very scientific principle, by making ridges of snow across the landing area, and expecting that, the wind and snow still continuing, drifts would be formed behind the ridges. Of course as soon as I finished, wind and snow stopped, but have just started again, otherwise I am still very well and walk out to the sports field twice a week. Luckily, the urge to play rugger has not struck me, so I only lose small chunks of my fingers on the hockey field.

March began with a minor medical setback:

My great work Goldfinches is having a rest at the moment as I have been warned off reading or writing too much, and for the last four days I have had headaches usually caused by sudden exertion or a change for darkness to brightness. But it is all improving rapidly, and I'll probably be back in the old rut shortly. Unfortunately I will not get it finished by the time I start watching again in spring. It would probably be a good idea in many ways to give intensive bird-watching a miss altogether this summer, but I am afraid opportunities will be scarce later so I'd better seize what I can get. On the other hand there won't be many opportunities to be lazy, which is something which also appeals to me.

It was one thing to devote all his waking hours to a vigil on a single nest when there was nowhere else to go. It was quite another to do so when it meant denying himself a daily two-hour release from his imprisonment on parole walks. When spring came, he enjoyed the simple pleasures of watching:

House sparrows were copulating on a fence. They did it 10 times in the first minute and 5 times in the last 45 seconds...

14th April
Within twenty four hours of putting up a nest box a pair of great tits began building. I put it up after lunch on 13th and they began building early this morning.

18th April
A common redstart has being going into the nest box which is occupied by the great tits which only succeeded in scolding the other birds. It remained in for c. 10 seconds.

He also, rather reluctantly, followed the example set by his former birdwatching companions, writing home on 27th April:

I've taken a rather saner view of life, and am carrying on much the same as usual, except for one indiscretion when I thought it might be a good idea to teach some of those

people who ask me questions about birds. Unfortunately I
did not repent of it in time, so I am bound to natter twice
a week on birds seen round the camp and on walks.

Conder settled on a plan for a rather less arduous nesting
season:

May 15th
I am not doing any really intensive bird watch this year,
only carrying out two rather smaller surveys; one a census
of all birds seen on walks in their different habitats and the
other a general survey of all the birds in the camp, so that
I have a definite object inside and outside the camp.

His resolve to do less was shattered within the week – a pair
of goldfinches had begun to nest within the camp. Buxton had
carried out two full seasons of watching redstarts; it would have
been a dereliction of duty for Conder not to have begun another
intensive watch to widen and deepen his own study. He denied
himself parole walks outside and sat at his post with despair
in his heart. It was with a palpable sense of relief that Conder
wrote home on 5th June:

My goldfinches have deserted, thank heavens so that I
haven't got that complication to worry me. As usual birds
take up much of my time though I am giving flowers a
tremendous going over. I have found and identified about
170 different species, but my friend, my preceptor, has got
about 100 more. He has the advantage of knowing what
he is looking for or knowing what he is looking at when

he is out. I only discover something when I have got back. My advantage is that he is rather long or short sighted, I forget which.

The following day, great things were happening on the Normandy beaches, as the D-Day landings began. In northern Germany, Conder was listening to perhaps the greatest mimic in the bird world – each male of the species samples the song of at least 75 other birds from both Europe and Africa in its repertoire: "A warbler, probably a marsh warbler, was singing from a group of hazels or other shrubs to the NW of the camp. It could imitate very well and a wryneck, great tit and thrush have been heard."

He celebrated an unwanted anniversary on 13th June with equanimity: "I'm in very good heart really, as I suppose might be expected, although this is the first day of my fifth year in 'jug'." At the beginning of July, he offered a glimpse into his inner thoughts:

I am still working quite hard, mostly at flowers, and old birds notes, and something rather new – "a diagnosis" of the effect that captivity has had upon people. During the last week I've been thinking about it, but haven't written anything. At present the very general impression is that we have changed mentally, though not unrecognisably by a long way. When we were about two years old we used to ask newcomers if they thought we had been affected by this, we don't do it any longer, but what that means I am not sure, but what has happened is that many of the civilised attractions or distractions are not available and we are thrown more upon our own resources, so that the growing up process has probably been speeded up. Also we question things more than we used to.

That summer, with birds thin on the ground, Conder turned his ultra-meticulous powers of observation on three sunflower plants. His quarry was a cluster of black aphids. The insects were themselves the quarry of a parasitic ichneumon wasp. As ever, no detail was spared: "14:29:45 begins to prick young aphids, 14:31:30 stops, withdraws ovipositor & starts looking for new host. 14:32:30 starts on an adult, which does not move." Thankfully, for the sake of space in his notebook, Conder broke off his aphid watch after three days to go housebuilding for the Swedish Red Cross representative, and when he returned, the aphids had gone.

Parole walks continued through August and one particular day provoked a sharp pang of homesickness in the prisoner:

At the moment, I am in a valley about a mile wide, the bottom of which is cultivated, with few trees except along the road so that I can see clearly across the valley to the hill. This is about six hundred feet high, covered with mixed coniferous and deciduous trees. Sometimes I imagine myself wandering amongst the scrub oak towards these trees, seeing the sky grow, until I am under the needles and can see what lies below. There I expect a view such as I would see on the North Downs, from a sandy range, over miles of rolling tree-strewn country, but I know I shall only be disappointed and see another hill like this.

Sadness was mixed with delight in the same week:

> I had a tremendous day out. There had been an arts and
> crafts exhibition at which the Commandant had been
> rather impressed and he promised to take them out for
> a day. The artists went to very attractive farms, and the
> others which included naturalists went for a long walk,
> and climbed a hill which we had long wished to do. It is
> the highest in the district, and is a war memorial for the
> whole of this area. It has a tower, like that on Leith Hill,
> which carries you above the tree tops. The view was good
> but it was unfortunately one of those hot, hazy days so
> that we did not get the full benefit of it. We had walked
> about the whole way through the forests, so that we were
> not very hot by the time we got to the farm, where we had
> food with the others. It is the prettiest farm in the district,
> a timbered house without a dung heap under the main
> window. Two ornate duck-ponds with masses of white
> ducks continually rippling the water under some weeping
> willows, and a very fresh lawn, and masses of sunflowers.
> We finished with a bathe in the river on the way home.
> Undoubtedly the best day I have had during the last four
> years.

Conder was among those prisoners willing to record their
experiences who fell under the supervision of a Cambridge
University tutor. Professor CJ Hamson, a law lecturer who had
been captured in Crete, encouraged them to write about their
captivity. Each prisoner received a wartime logbook from the
YMCA, complete with a quaint letter "to bring you greetings

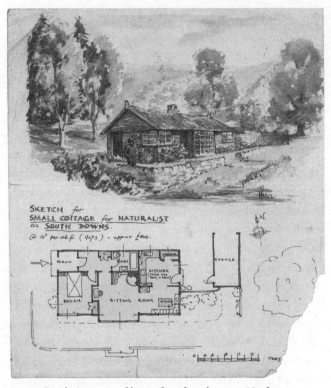

SKETCH for SMALL COTTAGE for NATURALIST on SOUTH DOWNS.

Conder's vision of home for after the war. No fences.

from friends and to facilitate your recording some of your experiences during these eventful years… If you are a poet, major or minor, confide your lyrics to these pages." Conder was inspired to begin keeping a daily record of his thoughts and feelings.

August 29th, 1944
This is the first entry of my diary, written in a prison camp, during I hope the last few months or weeks of

the war. After a long spell of hot sun, the weather has broken, and only once in the day, did I see the sun break thro' the clouds. The wind blew coolly from the west, and occasionally a light rain fell, tho' only in the afternoon. The temperature was just right for walking, and too cold for bathing, so that we walked up the road behind the camp – keeping our eye open for apples off the trees that line the roads, then branched off east up the hill into the forests, where we had earlier collected raspberries. We walked thro' the trees along the ridge till we came to what is known as "Bebia view", for from here, just over Rotenburg we look down towards Bebia. The intermediary plains are uninteresting for they are flat, and the corn has been cut so that the wind no longer ripples the corn and the rye. But behind Bebia the hills rise and the view is more interesting. In the haze of the distance I could just see the beginnings of Thuringian Wald. Most of the hills nearby are too utilitarian to be attractive. The summits are covered with planted forests, and the hillsides are cultivated up to the forest. There's little or no wild woodland as I remember it from Hurtwood*.

Like most newly purposeful diarists, Conder's resolve to keep a daily log soon fizzled out. He kept it up for just thirteen consecutive days, but in that brief period, he painted some of the most vivid word-pictures in the whole of his captivity. By

---

* On the North Downs where Conder had lived in his youth.

the end of August, he had shared the same room with the same nine men for more than a year, getting up with the same men, going to bed with them around him. The entries simmered with the petty tensions, alliances and conflicts among people who knew each other far too well, exemplified by his rocky friendship with his botanist buddy.

August 31
It is interesting to see the number of cliques in my room and how they fit and how they fail. The room is mostly divided into pairs of which I suppose the most noticeable is John Cripps and myself, and we are known as an example of a "perfect prison friendship".

The qualification for a "PPF" is that one must always be together.

But nothing is perfect. Within a week, Conder was telling his paper confidant:

I seem to have been in rather a bad temper recently, very short with John Cripps. I wonder whether my tooth, or at least the hole in my gum, which is clearing up slightly now, has been making me so sour. I seem to have lost my patience especially with him, and his usual jokes, very shallow ones, don't get their usual retorts, and when he does something wrong I get rather cross and tick him off, rather than talking to him as I used to, and consequently I put myself in the wrong too… to see him sniffing around me, watching what I do out of the corner of his eye, is rather like a red flag to me.

Over the next few days, Conder blew hot and cold as he and Cripps stumbled towards some kind of rapprochement.

The content of the diary makes it clear that the guards were no longer confiscating prisoners' notes for inspection, or even looking at them. A ruminative piece on 4th September offered a positive ending:

> I today contemplated two things; firstly to write out my ideas on God and my moral creed; and secondly to write an essay on nature, showing the way man treats it, firstly probing into it scientifically and secondly using it aesthetically, perhaps writing the 2nd one for the mushroom? I wonder if I will be able to get either of them done in time, for the news seems to be getting better and better.

The "news" was certainly getting better. The night before, they had heard on the camp radio that Paris had been liberated, British troops had crossed the Seine, the Americans had taken Avignon, and Romania had declared war on Germany. Yet nothing brought the impending reality of victory closer than the events taking place above the camp a week later:

> September 11th
> After the usual cold night and misty morning the sun came out, with some clouds coming down from the north. At about 10.30am the long distance air raid alarm went which was followed immediately by the close alarm, three minutes later 7 fighters with twin condensed streaks following each plane flew NE in a wide formation. All that we could see of them was a

silver point followed by this long white streak. Every few minutes these fighters passed over at a great height, and just after 11.00am the first flying fortress appeared, and in these you could see most of the details, the 4 engines etc, so that comparing them to the fighter you could get a good idea of their size. At this point I went to have my hair cut, but from the window I could still see the southern sky, and could see 3 flights coming up from the horizon mostly betrayed by their condense streaks before we could see the planes. More and more of these planes appeared sometimes in flights of 16,10 and up to 40 or 50, mostly shining in the sun, but some of them being blackish in colour. When the largest flight came over in perfect formation, a train full of trees and heavy AA guns was stationary on the line opposite the camp. Here was an AA gunner's dream, but their guns were immobilised. I bet they were cursing. We only saw 3 German fighters diving in and out amongst the clouds. I was inside when most of the exciting things happened, when a fighter fired some rockets into their planes directly overhead, missing the bombers and again when a bomber came down, and circled round and round whilst his crew jumped out, and then after a longish interval, the pilot himself, or they presumed it to be the pilot as their plane dived immediately after he had left, dropped out and floated down.

Swerving round and round the largest groups of bombers were our own fighters, guarding this great force. The planes continued to go over NE until about 1pm when some planes were seen coming back in a SW direction. During part of this display a softball game was being played which reached 15 innings, twice the length of a normal game. Both sides reached 6 all in the 7th innings and after that no more runs were scored until the 15th.

Though they did not know it, the prisoners had been watching the 8th US Air Force heading deep into the heart of eastern Germany. A hundred and thirty-two bombers struck at the arms factory in Chemnitz, near Dresden. Two days later, the jubilation con-tinued as another Allied force went overhead:

September 13th
The weather still holds and we had an even better air display than two days ago. The planes were evidently returning from a raid, and they came back from a NE direction, almost immediately over the camp. All in 400 bombers and fighters were counted. We could see the trails of condensing mist chucking up the sky from the horizon some time before we could see the planes. We saw two planes come down; one some distance away came down circling, and the other closer, obviously a German fighter as it had been attacking a bomber formation, which suddenly dived to the ground in a curve like a plummet gathering speed almost the whole time, in flames, or at least leaving a trail of white smoke behind it.

After most of the bombers had passed we had a dog fight to the S of the camp, and could see the planes diving, and circling just over the S hills, and were sometime able to hear guns firing. The G plane dived out of it and came roaring towards the camp at a tremendous speed.

After doing my botany lesson I had lain on the grass reading.

The squadrons that flew over that day gave hope to prisoners in more than one camp. A couple of hours before, they had targeted the synthetic oil plants at Blechhammer and Monowitz in Poland. Some stray bombs had landed close by, causing damage to another camp enclosed by barbed wire – Auschwitz.

Some of the concentration camp inmates were killed by the falling bombs, but so too were German soldiers. Camp survivor Shalom Lindenbaum remembered: "How beautiful was it to see squadron after squadron burst from the sky, drop bombs, destroy the buildings, and kill also members of the *Herrenvolk**... Those bombardments elevated our morale and, paradoxically, awakened probably some hopes of surviving, of escaping from this hell."

That autumn, there was little to enthuse the birdwatching prisoner. In October:

> I keep myself quite well occupied during most of the day reading up botany, entomology and ornithology, most of which is quite interesting. I am not taking too much exercise as scoff is getting rather short but play an occasional game of hockey. Walks stopped, as I think I told you some time ago, but may, I suppose be restarted some day, so that I can do practically no field work.

---

* The master race.

The parole walks never did restart; for the rest of the war, the prisoners were kept behind the barbed wire, apart from strictly guarded expeditions outside for wood cutting, providing fuel for their hut stoves. In November, Conder sought to keep himself active by embarking on an ornithological survey from within the camp. He decided to carry out two bird censuses; one of a small ploughed field just beyond the wire and the second, a blackthorn hedge at the back of the field. It made for an occupation of stupefying dullness in the most miserable weather. On the first day, he recorded with great diligence: "0850 5 piles of manure 1000 more manure 1335 still more manure 1614 17 piles of manure." One magpie was all he had to show for his field records in the first fourteen days. It was an exercise of either great perserverance or sheer masochism as he noted rain, snow or overcast skies on 48 days and just ten birds of four species. The hedge proved a little more productive, but only a little.

The day before he abandoned his seven-week survey, he wrote home. He could not have known that it would be the last letter his family would receive from him.

December 17 1944

During the last two or three days the weather has taken a turn for the better and is now rather colder but less rainy. I had been hoping to go out again last week to cut wood for the camp but a series of misfortunes occurred and so far nothing has come of it. I managed to get a bit more work done instead. I have just completed a paper on the difference in the habitat between two closely related birds which are common here but not so common in England [common and black redstarts]. Most of it is I am afraid rather hypothetical. I have just finished a chapter on plant ecology in German which was very interesting. After Christmas I am going to get down to Botany in a big way as I have just discovered two quite good books. But I won't really be able to get going until I have finished two more bird papers, one rather hypothetical on physical sensitivity in birds, and another on the results of a census I took on walks during the summer and winter months. During this winter I am watching birds of the camp and the results might be quite interesting and to complete the picture I have lessons on insects 2 or 3 times a week. Consequently you can see that I have got much too much to occupy myself and gone are the days when I used to take things easily whilst lying on my bed. In spite of this urge to work and the idea that to work is to get near happiness, sometimes I crave for the good old days.

Best wishes for Christmas 1944 Oflag IX AZ

HAPPY NEW YEAR?

The bombers drum their way along the night
With slow tattoo, down an invisible track
Drawn on a map of Europe, which now lies black,
Huddled in silence. So, at mountain-height,
They tread their level path beyond our sight
And pass relentlessly onward, flinging back
The tramp of engines moving to attack
Enemy cities, to set their streets alight.
And we lie listening, hoping to hear the burst
Of bombs in the crumbling houses, to hear the panes
Shivering in our windows. We shall be first
To tot up the dead in the papers. (Someone explains
That this is a partial list.) We too have been cursed
By the bombs; we have felt their pulses in all our veins.

John Buxton, Sonnet 14

The new year at Eichstätt began with an empty canteen noticeboard. John Buxton had stopped the ritual of pinning up the weekly nature report in mid-December, a tradition that had stretched back to August 1943. Perhaps ritual implied permanence and he wanted to break with anything that suggested life would go on as before. If the previous year had started with the hope that the war would end, this one was palpably the beginning of the end. On all points of the compass, the Wehrmacht was in retreat. The last German offensive, a push into the Ardennes that gained the name of the Battle of the Bulge, was now being repulsed, Budapest had fallen to Soviet troops and, on the Saar, the Allies had made their first incursion into pre-war German territory.

On a practical level, all communication with the outside world ended on the last day of December and food was once again running short, bringing memories of the early days at Laufen. The camp had seen a big influx of displaced POWs from the east, adding to overcrowding in the damp, now mould-ridden huts, and January brought heavy snowfalls and plunging temperatures. On 14th February, Buxton registered his yearning to leave in a letter to Marjorie that would receive no reply:

> A wonderful bright day today and the 1st larks singing – as they shd since it is St Valentine's. How I long to be able to take a walk in a straight line more than 300 yards where I like, and to watch the birds. Shall I be home in time to go to see the Shearwaters, or to find a Redstart somewhere near LC [Long Crendon, their Buckinghamshire home]? If not perhaps we can go to look at the dunlins and godwits at the estuary.

Even as the worst of winter abated, the men were suffering a double imprisonment. In March, there were 54 air raid alarms at the camp. Each time the sirens sounded, the prisoners were confined to their barracks. One man was shot dead standing at the door of his hut; the prisoner who went to pick him up was killed too.

Buxton began an unlikely and clandestine friendship with one of his guards. Wilhelm von Cornides had seen and experienced too much. As a 22-year-old Wehrmacht officer in Czechoslovakia, he had looked into cattle trucks crammed with women and children, and, chatting to railway policemen in attendance, had learned about their destiny – bound for the gas chambers of Chelmo. Cornides had then endured battle on the Eastern Front and was decorated for bravery. Now a wounded veteran at 24, seeing out the war as a camp guard, he told Buxton he wished the bombs would rain down on his morally bankrupt homeland as a kind of cleansing purgatory. The listening prisoner felt no sense of moral superiority: fellow librarian Dorrien Belson remembered a suppressed anger in Buxton at that time, which poured out in one of his most bitter anti-war poems, "The Prisoners", written in February 1945. It contained the lines:

Shall we stop the mouths of fools for future wars concocting rules?
Or will our memory disdain to speak, until war come again?

Buxton recalled that in those last months of the war there was no slackening of discipline within the prisoners' ranks. The men had to be prepared for cooperative resistance should SS soldiers enter the camp and order a massacre, or be ready to give assistance to invading parachutists. They dreaded the thought of being sent south into the Alps, because they doubted that they would survive the journey.

Nor was there any slackening in birdwatching, though it was harder to spend any sustained period of time outside with the repeated and irregular interruptions from air raids. Buxton faithfully noted the first arrivals of the spring: a starling building its nest on 21st March, the first willow warbler on 3rd April, a wood warbler on 5th, a tree pipit singing in the woods on the next day. It was the last entry in Buxton's bird-recording notebook.

Later that week, Buxton went into the camp hospital with an intestinal complaint. Lying in his bed, he could hear the sound of distant guns. A lifelong diarist whose records had been interrupted by the war, he resolved now to break his long self-imposed silence as a prisoner: "The tedium and frustrations of those five years, four of them in Bavaria and one in Westphalia, did not seem to be worth recording in a diary, quite apart from the risk of inadvertent disclosures if a diary were found during the frequent searches to which we were subjected." But things were different now. The camp guards had long since abandoned any efforts at examining what any prisoners wrote, so Buxton had a certain amount of liberty to record for posterity what he knew would be momentous times ahead. On the sixth anniversary of his marriage, he picked up his pen:

April 12th 1945, Eichstätt. In hospital since 7th. The march out ordered for Saturday 14th at 5am – the first definite orders so I thought I would begin this diary of our journey. I shall presumably be on the march as the latest news is that only four are to stay. However, von Cornides told me this evening that... I ought to as I didn't look well... I'd prefer to go if we go, though I realise I'm not fit to march, and may not get far. Von Cornides said he thought we were going to Moosburg [a POW camp to the west], which at least will mean food. And owing to numbers there (said to be 70–100,000) a further move is perhaps less likely, and relief there should not be long delayed.

I spent the afternoon packing up books etc, and a suitcase full of letters. I wonder how much of it we'll see again. My original verse MSS and transcripts of those not known to have reached home I carry till I drop. Also some 23lbs of food. Von Cornides says he'll bring me some oatmeal; I feel I could live on porridge.

Two chaotic days of packing and "will we won't we go" followed, before Buxton – dosed up with opium pills – and the other sick prisoners waited for the arrival of motorised transport and watched the able-bodied being marched out of the camp with pride in their steps early one morning. The tail end of the column was still queuing at the gate when eight American Thunderbolt fighter aircraft strafed the prisoners on the road with gunfire. When the aircraft had gone, Buxton rushed out to do what he could and in his diary gave a picture of the chaos and destruction they had caused:

I returned and carried out blackboards etc. to help carry in the wounded. Some walked in and I washed a few, and we carried down beds, fetched blankets, brought in kit and so on. Ten of ours were killed, and of c.50 wounded, nine, we know, had had amputations by Saturday night [14th April

– Buxton wrote this entry two days later]. Von Cornides is said to have got up out of a ditch during the raid to bring Denison into shelter after he was hit. Some took refuge in the cellars of the water-house and a girl there dressed someone's wound in the leg. Gordon Diack's sporran was shot off as he ran across the field. Sandy Jamieson and others jumped into the river. Jacko somehow came back with eight eggs. An American airman next to Jo Henry (whose hand got a graze) said, "Now I know what it's like to be in the army." "Emma" Hamilton was seen coming out of a cave with two German girls: one of them shook her head and said "*Sehr kalt!*"* and laughed. The women in the Married Quarters were very good helping. All the wounds were from .55 gunfire. No bombs were dropped on the column.

That night, under cover of darkness, Buxton was one of 25 sick men who climbed into a truck to be towed by a tractor. They arrived at the POW camp of Moosburg after "a nine hour journey of c.60 km, and somewhat nerve-wracking after the experience of the previous morning, especially after it grew light… There are some 2,500 men here, in very bad huts – worse than Warburg or Aldershot – and extremely crowded. It is full of lice, bugs and fleas, and the water supply amounts to (at most) one tap for 300… I fell asleep in the compound, not having slept for 36 hours."

---

* Very cold.

Here, the men encountered one of the American pilots who had shot at their fellow prisoners as they walked out of Eichstätt. He justified his action by claiming he thought he was shooting at German troops: "You were marching. POWs don't march; they slouch."

Offered a wet, stinking mattress soiled by a victim of dysentery, Buxton half-slept on the ground instead and endured dreadful days in which he was plagued with diarrhoea, able to eat only porridge and biscuits. With nothing to do but wait, the men of all nationalities sat in the open all day, lighting fires and boiling billies of tea and coffee, while war raged all around. Buxton looked out one evening at a pall cast over far-off Regensburg, "a vast, still bank of brown smoke". New arrivals continued to pour into the camp, including RAF men from Sagan, ragged and exhausted after a march of several hundred miles.

Buxton fretted over the absence of contact with his wife:

I have had no letter from her written this year. I hope she doesn't know of the strafing last Saturday. One of the RAF at Sagan had a letter: "This is the last letter you will have from me, as I am going to marry one of the heroes of 1944 instead of one of the cowards of 1940." Of course, we have had plenty of this sort of thing.

April 21st A very bad day. Masses of planes, including fighter sweeps this morning which set my heart racing madly, argue as I will with myself. I fell asleep at the table after lunch, and slept almost all the afternoon… I ought to write a fuller account of all this but, though much better today (22nd) I can't: the last 36 hours are best forgotten.

Americans flooded out of their tents by a thunderstorm
came into this hut to sleep.

April 22nd Cold and windy, but I feel I've begun to
pull myself together again, I suppose this nervous state is
natural enough – others are worse than I – but it seems
deplorably near to a cowardly break-down.

Two days later, Buxton had recovered some of his health and
spirits, and it proved to be the prelude to the liberation he had
been awaiting for just short of five years.

April 24th Wandered round with John [Leighton-Boyce]
this afternoon and sat looking at the wood to the north,
listening to willow warblers and tree pipits... Many guards
going off this afternoon with full kit. Excitement rises, as
well it might.

April 25th Hardly slept owing to excitement and
discomfort: some internal, but also noise of guns to west,
bed-boards falling on my head, John's feet prodding the
top of my head etc... At 3p.m. Jack Higgon [Lt Col JHV
Higgon] read out a statement issued by a conference of
Senior Allied Officers here with the senior International
Red Cross man. No further movement of POWs from
camp; only a skeleton German staff to be left for the sake
of certain formalities; the camp to be under the unified
command of the Senior Allied Officer (Group Captain
Willets); all supplies to be shared out equally among all.
The Commandant had not yet had confirmation, but to
all intents and purposes the camp is now under Allied
command. First swift of the year this pm.

An air of excited unreality hung around the camp. The following day:

> I went out collecting wood near the R. Isar, a swift, glacier-grey river like the Salzach at Laufen. We went to a farm-house and got a (small) hunk of bread, but we had been preceded by too many Americans. The old peasant who gave it to us asked, as usual, how long the war would last, and was incredulous and shocked when I said "Not more than ten days". I was out for about two hours in very pleasant country, but all seems to be a dream now – buying bread off German peasants in open farming country among the fresh green of spring, while overhead fly our aircraft, as low as they please, looking for anything moving, to destroy it.

But as the wait ran into May with no signs of any moves towards repatriation, snow fell and the prisoners were on little more than soup rations, for American soldiers had stolen all the bread that was meant for them. Officers who had been given passes went to the town of Moosburg and returned with stories of GIs looting and raping civilians.

On the first of the month, Buxton wrote: "At c.3.40pm, a whisper went round that General Patton was in camp. I went up to the Lagerstrasse and saw him, standing up in a jeep, in tin hat, battle-dress, and with a breastful of ribbons. He visited a tent and spoke conventional congratulations on our bearing in these circumstances. He drove back slowly, standing up and saluting, with a much beringed hand."

A drop-in visit from the conquering hero of the US Third Army was all very well. Other things moved John Buxton more deeply:

A willow-warbler
(Moosburg, Germany, May 2nd, 1945: relieved April 29th)

I may walk in the woods now
Where the spears of grass
Thrust through the fallen leaves, and rain
Spills from the trees I pass.
I need not wait now till you come near
Nor grieve when you go where I cannot hear.

I may stand in the woods now
And lean by a tree.
Your fairy laughter I hear again;
In the breaking leaves I see
Where you go flitting above my head,
Free to follow wherever I'm led.

Nearly a week later, Buxton secured a pass to go out of the camp, and, though he did not know it then, he went into the German countryside for the last time. The object of his final recorded observations was so very apt: "Plenty of redstarts about, singing and ticking in the woods and orchards."

On the afternoon of VE Day (8th May) Buxton and his companions were flown to Rheims in France. It was two days short of five years since he had been captured. But they had to wait one more night; all the aircrews took the rest of the day off to celebrate victory in Europe: "Slept on a camp bed in a tent of fourteen – the least crowded quarters I've slept in for five years. A nightingale singing all through the night quite near – not a very good one, but a lovely welcome out of Germany."

THE NOT-SO-GREAT ESCAPE

There was little to raise Peter Conder's spirits in the first months of 1945. All correspondence with the outside world had ceased, a dreadful blow in the depths of winter, and Conder's own meticulous record-keeping ran out too. He made up a chart for "Birds of Rotenburg am Fulda January 1945", but, uncharacteristically, the entries were incomplete, stopping short at 4th January with a smattering of crows and sparrows.

Conditions were becoming grim in the camp. Allied victories blocked lines of communication through Germany, so that Red Cross parcels no longer got through. Prisoners and captors alike were beginning to go hungry. It is quite possible that the men passed most of those winter days lying in their bunks. Conder gained some bitter amusement from watching two British Army chaplains come to unchristian blows over some scraps of food.

The last week of March 1945 saw the Allied armies advance with great speed through Germany. Fifteen bridgeheads spanned the Rhine in just 48 hours. On 27th March, Winston Churchill wrote: "A beaten army not long ago Master of Europe retreats before its pursuers." On the same day, the German officers at Rotenburg were debating what to do with their charges.

All of the prisoners harboured the feeling that they could be killed at any time, and there is no doubt that they were genuinely in danger from some quarters. Feldwebel Heinrich Sultan, a former janitor of the school, and by then a sergeant at the camp, recalled one officer standing up to say: "*Meine Herren, es möge jetzt kommen wie es will, bevor die Kriegsgefangenen den Amerikanern in die Hände fallen, werden sie alle umgelegt.*" ("Gentlemen, whatever happens, before the POWs can fall into the hands of the Americans, they will all be killed"). Sultan portrayed his own role in the discussion as that of one who stood in heroic disagreement. His final comment, however, has a realistic ring of pragmatism: "*Schiessen tut keiner mehr, das ist vorbei. Der Krieg ist verloren, und da können wir nicht auch noch 500 Menschen hier umlegen.*" ("Nobody is going to shoot any more, all that is in the past. The war is over and we cannot just kill another 500 people.")

The German authorities at Rotenburg were actually well prepared, in spite of shortages, for a measured evacuation of the camp. They had been gathering provisions for some weeks, so that on 28th March, sixteen horses and two trucks set off along a forest track. The prisoners were told to pack their bags, and followed the convoy an hour later. Conder remembered:

> As we were marched out of our camps we could carry very little. I took only my most treasured possessions – basic clothes for the journey, the notebooks in which I had written my Goldfinch observations, a bird diary and one book – A *Daily Telegraph* Miscellany edited by JB

Firth and published in 1940 and which 50 years later I still have.

Fourteen-year-old Bjorn Ulf Noll, the son of a teacher who had taught at Rotenburg when the camp was still a school, had stayed on in the civilian quarters. He paints a vivid picture of the evacuation:

> It was a cloudy midday. All Oflagists had rucksacks on, carried satchels or at least had only a minimum of necessary things to ease transportation. They more or less looked like refugees not being allowed to carry more than some kilograms... All of the men's dress-order seemed to me comparatively sloppy... opened jackets, unbuttoned coats, but with their officers' caps like on formal duty. And they marched in a rather lame or at least unmilitary way – as if they were convinced about the futility of that progress. Where before they had been used to being kept tightly together by an assortment of watch-towers, they now, at least to me, seemed to be free from rifled guards. It looked as if they were following their own intentions rather than the militarised standards of that time.

The men tried to barter for the boy's handcart with cigarettes, but it was not his to give. Two weeks later, American forces would steal it from his family.

The trek began. Townspeople spat at the prisoners as they passed their houses. Very quickly the column began to stretch out. Ernest Edlmann wrote in his diary: "Very slow pace and frequent halts – all very tired and weak". Peter Conder was marching alongside his friend John Cripps. They passed down a track through some beech woods and as they went round a bend, the two men realised that they were temporarily out of sight of the guards. They made a break for the trees and kept going, even when voices shouted "*Halt!*" behind them. Perhaps they expected a bullet in the back. But nobody fired and nobody gave chase. Much later, Feldwebel Sultan noted that seven men had escaped on that first day. Edlmann noticed that the guards generally turned a blind eye to these dashes for freedom, and escaped himself a day or two later. Even some of the guards slipped away into the woods to bring an end to their war.

The two escapees knew none of this and were in fear for their lives. That night, they slept out in the forest and in the darkness were terrified when they heard the sound of barking dogs. The dogs came no closer, though, and after a while the fugitives realised that the "dogs" were in fact barking deer.

At daybreak, the two men pressed on and, much to their relief, reached a farmhouse that they recognised from their parole walks. They crept into one of the outbuildings but were discovered. However, the farmer offered bread, not bullets, for he was an anti-Nazi, a former army major of the Great War who was already sheltering more than twenty POWs and political dissidents. His wife fed the men and offered them coffee. John Cripps downed fifteen cups and was violently sick.

Conder and Cripps slept in a barn on the farm for four or five nights. Battle raged around them now – bombardments from artillery and then the crack of gunfire. On the last morning, they could hear lorries and tanks rumbling close by the farmhouse. Fearing the German army was approaching, Conder looked outside and saw something he had never seen before in his life – black soldiers driving lorries. The Americans had arrived.

The US infantrymen took the two men to a military hospital. A nurse riled them by saying scornfully: "You should see some of our boys." Conder and Cripps hitched a ride on the back of an American tank towards France. It was exactly five years since a boy just out of his teens had marched through rich, verdant countryside. A man entering his late twenties now passed shattered buildings and bombed landscapes on his way home.

THE LONG MARCH

An eastern weather front reached Sagan in time for Christmas 1944, bringing deep snow to the camp. The Eastern Front itself was advancing at that time too… in a westerly direction. Red Army troops rode on US-manufactured troop carriers, moving up to 50 or 60 miles a day, the Wehrmacht holding strategic towns and cities, but elsewhere in headlong retreat. Towards the end of January, the POWs could hear the boom of approaching Russian guns. The commanding officers ordered Red Cross parcel contents to be eaten at once instead of being rationed, and prisoners began exercising, walking round and round the perimeter, preparing their skinny, malnourished bodies for evacuation.

John Barrett and Barney Thompson held earnest discussions about what to do with their bird notes. On the face of it, Barrett made the careful and rational decision, justified in his autobiography 50 years later: "In days soon to come I might have to choose between carrying a tin of bully beef or my tree sparrow monograph. So I packed that superb addition to ornithological understanding as tight as I could, addressed it to myself in England in four languages." The postman must have understood only a fifth language, for Barrett never saw his work again.

Barney could not bear to part with nearly two years of his life. He placed his notebooks and the newspaper-wrapped crested lark wings at the very bottom of his bag, so that any later weakness of spirit on his part would see the contents at the top jettisoned first.

On a snowy night when the temperature fell below minus ten degrees, the order was given to march. And was greeted with disbelief. Barney's diary, scribbled on cigarette packets and scraps of paper at the end of each day, gives a vivid and immediate account of chaos and hardship:

27.1.45 Warning given at 8pm to be ready to march at 10pm. Big flap. Not regarded seriously at first, then preparations started with gt speed. Kits packed – everything reduced to minimum – one change of clothing, blankets & as much food as possible & I took most essential notebooks. Heartbreaking to see all the books which are left, not to mention piles of clothes – almost anything could have been picked up, for no one could carry much.

Just before 10 readiness put off to 1.45, then later to 23.59, 0030, & finally 0700. On this we tried to sleep & got in 3-4 hrs. Food we could not carry was "bashed" or made unusable. Lined up in camp at 0700 & were ages getting away. Packs felt v. heavy. People with sledges well off – these made during flap overnight.

28.1.45 Left camp at approx 0930 after collecting food parcel. Americans had jettisoned huge amt. food – Klim, prunes, cigarettes, salmon, sardines, laying in piles on snow. We picked up a lot & threw much into Russian compound. Russians threw out matches & gave us a good send off.*

March was at slow pace in strong icy cold wind, occasional snow, but I found it very tiring with pack which seemed to weigh a ton.

Route at first was SW through pines, pines, pines. Occasional breaks with usual monotonous flat agricultural country. Stopped at midday in biting wind & quickly froze up – ate salmon & sardines, oil freezing up as we ate.

Reached Halbau c. 1530 some 18 mls from Sagan & stood around in cold for 4 hrs – until finally billeted in school – v. crowded & general chaos. Slept in very crowded conditions 70 to a room, in corridors etc. Difficult handling kit & trying to sort out food with a crowd jostling all around & stepping all over one & one's belongings. V. tired & slept none the less. Surprised to hear from Jimmy.**

(en route): – Many Cr. Tits, blue tits & goldcrests in pines, much calling. Rooks & Hoodies frequent. By villages tree sps. & Y.B's*** common, high % of latter males with strong head markings, magpie (1–2), chaffinch, singles seen several times, Duck – 2 nr. Sagan. Gt. Tits nr. Houses. I Gn Wdpkr at Holbau.

---

* The Russian POWs were left behind since the otherwise evacuated camp would be overrun by the Russian army.

** "Jimmy" was the illicit camp radio. Prisoners could say, quite innocuously "Jimmy says…" A group of men had brought it on the march.

***Yellow buntings i.e. yellowhammers.

One of Thompson's messmates, a New Zealand flight lieutenant called Tim Dooley, retained an image from the first day of the march: "At one of the stops, Barrett was offered some stew by a woman in one of the wagons. She said 'We are all the same now, you must take it, we have no country and no homes and are all cold and tired.'"

On that first night, John Barrett slept in the chapel of a nunnery along with 600 others. The sisters took down the crucifix and candles from the altar so that he and three fellow officers could stretch out and rest there.

* * *

For the next two days, friend and foe alike walked through a kind of hell in ice. The frozen roads were filled with soldiers and streams of refugees, many of whom had already walked for weeks. When the refugees' carthorses fell in their shafts through exhaustion, they were butchered in minutes. Barney recalled fleeting impressions of the trek:

30.1 A hard march – a lot of uphill work & bad weather – wind & thick snow. One particularly bad patch as we passed an aerodrome – snow blinding us, wind fierce, pretty well puckered out, but still staggered on. Took v little notice of surroundings – main idea being to keep eyes on sledge in front & keep pulling, but did peep across into the snow here & noticed 2 Me 109s [Messerschmitt fighter planes] & a twin job, probably a Hs 129 [Henschel anti-tank aircraft] & soon after heard a redwing call v.

loudly from a pine over my head – the whole trip is a recollection of odd things like this.

Thermometers had dropped below minus twenty. One
German guard lost a leg to frostbite, a Polish officer a foot. An
order was whispered around the men that anyone falling out
of line would be shot. But who would enforce it? In his diary,
Barney wrote: "We had expected strong guards, terror tactics,
trigger-happy Postens [guards] – instead a lot of very fed up,
exceedingly tired, footsore Goons trailed along among us."

Some of the older German guards were struggling to keep
up. In an act of extraordinary compassion, Barrett, the senior
Allied officer in the line, carried one guard's rifle for him and
ordered some of his fitter companions to carry other stricken
officers' weapons. They did so without objection.

Barney observed "opportunities for escape limitless" but
nobody did. The Allied airmen knew that many within the
civilian population viewed them very differently from their
army and navy colleagues. They had become demonised by the
German people as "*Kindermörder*", terror bombers who had
killed thousands of innocents in towns and cities. Gun-toting
boy soldiers of the Hitler Youth were among those who had
lynched grounded airmen. The POWs marched with the fear
of some kind of retribution, and here was an odd reversal of
roles: their guards had now turned from oppressors to protec-
tors, albeit dejected and enfeebled ones.

Three days into the march, there was a slight thaw and the
men stopped unexpectedly for the day at the town of Muskau
(and saw a covey of five partridges):

> Much trading going on mainly via German children.
> Some of these v. cute & delighted to get chocolate – hard
> to convince them that we really will give choc. for bread…
> Overhauled kit in view of thaw, as carrying seems likely in
> future… hung on to my notebooks.

Just 90 minutes before midnight, the column was split up.
Barrett stayed behind. Thompson found himself among the
contingent that was sent off on a night march out into the
unknown:

> Just struggled along somehow, falling asleep whilst walking
> and recovering as I found myself swaying out of line, and
> as soon as we halted dropping asleep in the slushy snow by
> the roadside. Time meant nothing & the only thing that
> one wanted to do was to lay down & sleep.

They trudged on for 24 hours until they reached some
railway sidings. Late at night, the dispirited men, exhausted
by a 60-mile march, squeezed into filthy cattle trucks. Barney
Thompson had "few hoodies, magpies, a sp. hawk & usual small
birds" to sustain him. Two sleepless nights in a windowless truck
were not enough to stop him peering through a narrow slit to
clock up three bullfinches, three jays and a buzzard plucking
its prey.

John Barrett, meanwhile, kept no notes and had no recollections of the week in which he was marched to the POW camp
at Luckenwalde, "the mud so deep, passage of refugees so awful
to see, that perhaps my memory could not contain the terror".
It is impossible now to imagine five million people wandering

around Germany in a permanent state of fear, desperation and bewilderment. He described Luckenwalde as "an abominable place with sordid, hungry overcrowding". Twenty-seven thousand prisoners occupied a camp built for 15,000. Almost apologetically, he would confess to Barney: "My bird notes in that place were only arrival dates. There was no migration of finches, larks, corvidae as at Sagan. I added nothing new to the lists." And when the German guards slipped away on 20th April, men of the Russian army became Barrett's new captors. High-level negotiations between Churchill and Stalin included discussions about what to do with the prisoners. If Britain and the US were to become the new enemy, the Soviets did not want to release 2,000 trained aircrew. Barrett whiled away the time teaching Polish officers English and captained the "England" chess team to victory against Norway. A full week after the end of war in Europe, the Russians allowed him to walk out of the camp gates for the day into the countryside nearby, a parody of a parole walk:

> Golden orioles were common but hard to see well. I found a tawny pipit pair that were possibly brooding; the nest eluded me. Several hoopoes in the area and in an alder by a ditch a pair of ortolan buntings – magnificent views of both birds.
>
> Those walks however were spoiled by dead bodies in the woods, masses of smashed equipment and all the litter and smelly remains of war & despair.

American lorries rolled up to relieve the camp on 20th May, and two days later Barrett was at "the US depot at

Halle, beautiful with flowering shrubs, sweet briar hedges & deep green groves of trees. There I found hawfinches being fed; heard so many nightingales singing together by day that I at once thought of the song from that party of arrived robins at Schubin. Such song I'd never heard before and it extended over three days at least". He never heard the end of that song, for Barrett hitched a flight to Brussels and was on his way home.

Barney Thompson's 48-hour train journey in early February took him through the city of Hannover – where his brother had been shot down, though he would not have known that at the time – and eventually to the naval POW camp at Tarmstedt. Two months later, with the camp full of wheatears, the men were sent on the march again: "Mass of bird song in open parkland type country near camp – best I have heard since a Kriegie." Skylarks and woodlarks were singing overhead, but elation turned to group dejection as the men were marched from place to place to avoid the liberating Allies, mostly sleeping out in the open. At one point, military police ordered them to walk down into a clay pit. The officers refused, sensing that they were being set up to be massacred. Barney did not record this in his daily notes – as the days went on, extraneous material vanished until he reported virtually nothing but birds, one cheering constant left in his life. On St George's Day, he saw, for the first time in his life, "storks nesting... Display by throwing head up back and over until beak vertical and head reversed". It was a red letter day, of sorts.

On the first night of May, he slept in a hayloft at Wulmenau and woke in surroundings that were "peaceful and beautiful

– hard to appreciate the war is over". The men waited on a "well pranged" aerodrome at Diepholz, where Barney found eleven species all singing very strongly. And then he was up in the air and bound for Brussels.

"The look in your eyes"

All of these young men had gone off to war. Who were the strangers returning to peace?

On 6th April 1945, well over five years after he had left to fight, Peter Conder returned to Britain and was taken straight to a military hospital. Immediately, it seems, he looked for some kind of normality and found it walking alone in the hospital grounds. He took out a notebook and pencil and began to list:

Stratton St Margaret
Field which had some form of root crop, but which has not been cleared this year.
Greenfinches calling 56, Yellowhammers, Linnets 2, Hedge Sparrow, Chaffinch, Swallow, Starling, Woodpigeons, 2 ladybirds (different species), ? field mouse.

After medical checks, he was returned to his family. The relatives of these long-lost soldiers did not know how to greet them. Conder's messmate Vincent Hollom was presented with £50 by his uncle "to make up for your lost youth". Natalie Conder met her brother off the train:

There was a kind of awkwardness really. He hadn't got a home any more. You felt awful for him; he had nothing to go to. We were all dying to ask him 'what happened, what did you do?' but we didn't. We all held back. Some instinct told us not to ask.

Research carried out in the US indicated that more than half of all POWs suffered from some form of post-traumatic stress. The evidence is very strong that Peter Conder was having some difficulties adapting to his new surroundings. He stayed only a few days with his father and the stepmother he had never met before and now did not like, before decamping to move in with his sister. Natalie had married the Vienna-born stand-up comedian Vic Oliver, a celebrity in 1940s Britain who had been the first castaway on *Desert Island Discs* three years before. The couple fed Peter well and he responded by being sick, unable to cope with rich food.

The unsettled, withdrawn soldier left to join the army of occupation in Europe and, at one point, went birdwatching in the Netherlands with his old POW friend John Barrett.

By the time he was demobbed in April 1946, a little balance and a sense of purpose had been restored to his life. He returned to the family advertising agency, stuck it out for all of ten days, then walked in to his father's office and said "I'm leaving".

Conder went back to stay with his sister at her flat in Westminster Gardens. Often, he would head for the British Library to sit writing up bird notes and papers. At other times, he would sit at the window, looking out. The acute observational skills he had honed in camp came into play. Natalie recalled: "We were eight floors up and he could see all these birds below.

They were all, you know, boring London birds." A man habitu-
ated to occupying a small space among a crowd, Conder would
have been acutely aware of the need for each man to have his
own personal space. Watching the behaviour of the gulls down
below, as well as tufted ducks in St James's Park, Conder began
to see patterns of behaviour; that in the case of these birds, the
space between was measurable. He coined the scientific phrase
"individual distance" – the minimum distance within which
an individual animal would tolerate another of the same species
without evasive action or conflict. The concept of "individual
distance" is still used by biologists today.

Meanwhile, the redundant advertising executive needed
some kind of employment. He hung on in London through
the winter of 1946, awaiting funding for a government-backed
research post under HN Southern into tawny owls. But in the
spring of 1947, money was still not forthcoming. Long-time
mentor John Buxton stepped in, persuading him to apply for
the post of voluntary warden on Skokholm. He was the only
candidate. Patricia Higginson, the supply officer for the island,
remembered a shy man who arrived at Dale Fort on the mainland and said little. He stared at people from under his hat –
out of nervousness, she thought. When he left on the boat for
Skokholm, he was looking for peace in solitude.

* * *

Held overlong by the "liberating" Russian army, even though
the war was finished, Squadron Leader John Barrett cadged a
lift in a Dakota to be reunited with his wife, daughter and the
three-year-old son he had never seen. He had been promoted to

wing commander two years before… though nobody had told him. On 29th June, he wrote to Barney Thompson: "Once safely home, where do you think I went? Did you say "Hickling"?* Yes, that's right – to the bearded tits and Montagu's harriers, the bitterns, yellow wags and so many more."

Thompson himself went on a journey of release a few days later, a kind of homage to his dead brother. He embarked on a 400-mile cycle ride to look for red kites in their last bastion within the mountains of mid-Wales, a journey his brother had taken alone in the summer of 1940, while Barney was bomber training abroad. Peter Thompson had failed in his quest, though with 80 bird species and tuberous pea on his tally, it was a wonderful failure. Barney struck lucky: *Mirabile dictum*, really saw the KITES – 2 gliding close along hillside."

His next self-appointed mission was to visit the families of his own dead aircrew mates, to tell them the story of what had happened. In Northern Ireland, he consoled the widow of his wireless operator, and, in due course, he married her. Barney Thompson did not become a professional conservationist. A planning officer in local government, he saved his life-affirming passion for birds for his spare time and remained, until late in life, a modest and committed volunteer for the Northants Wildlife Trust.

John Barrett stuck with the RAF for two more years and, in that time, did wonders for wildlife conservation. He "requisitioned" materials from an RAF store to help the Yorkshire Naturalists' Union set up a bird observatory at Spurn Point,

---

* *Hickling Broad, a Norfolk Naturalists' Trust reserve.

used a staff car to survey East Yorkshire for the British Trust for Ornithology rook census and (rather more dubiously) used a flight training session to fly up and down the Severn estuary on an aerial twitch after a lesser white-fronted goose was reported, at that time only the third ever seen in Britain. His reconnaissance completed, he biked over to the likely spot and watched the goose from a wartime pillbox at a certain place called Slimbridge, until two men stepped inside, one of whom was a certain naval officer called Peter Scott. The goose laid a golden egg, for Scott was to set up the Wildfowl Trust at that very site in the following year.

Tired of temporary postings within the RAF, Barrett decided to look for a permanent base for his growing family. He was about to apply to become artist Eric Ennion's assistant at a new field studies centre at Flatford Mill, when John Buxton alerted him to an opportunity in Pembrokeshire, where Ronald Lockley had re-established the bird observatory on Skokholm.

Through the West Wales Field Society, Lockley had secured funding for a field studies centre post at the old fort of Dale. He advised Barrett to resign his RAF commission and apply. It was nearly disastrous. Barrett arrived for interview full of self-belief, under-prepared and overconfident: "Barrett was quite unimpressive and did not try to convince the Committee that he was a suitable man." Only when the successful candidate had to turn the job down because of family illness did the interview panel go back to Barrett. Even then, they gave him a vote of little confidence by appointing him as acting assistant warden –there was no warden to assist! Nevertheless, that autumn he wrote from Dale Fort Field Centre to his old friend, Barney Thompson: "You need not bother about any more change of address. I'm here for good. It's far too lovely ever to leave." Barrett was as good as his word. He was to remain in Pembrokeshire for the rest of his long life.

* * *

Well before his pals returned from Germany, George Waterston appeared to have been having a high old time. Not quite. Robert Waterston remembered it took a good six months before his exuberant brother returned to "his old self". From his POW camp, John Buxton was hopeful of a future for Waterston, writing to Marjorie: "If he can get well he will do much, I'm sure and I have much faith in him and wish him all success and that someday I might help him in some ways (though I won't want to live on Fair Isle)."

As Waterston sat in hospital convalescing after a second kidney operation in the spring of 1944, ornithologist James Fisher paid him a visit and made him an offer of an eighteen-month contract with the British Trust for Ornithology, to commence once he had received his discharge papers from the army. In the meantime, once he had recovered sufficiently, Waterston rattled out a torrent of letters to all and sundry, including Stresemann. That was a step too far for British military intelligence. They pursued him on the grounds that nobody could possibly be writing to a German in Berlin about birds.

Waterston started work for the BTO in September and, within a few weeks, wrote to George Stout on Fair Isle: "The work is proving intensely interesting and just suits me down to the ground. I am making a survey of the rooks and wood pigeons in North Aberdeenshire... I cover a wide area in my car and meet all sorts of grand characters – ghillies, foresters, game-keepers, farmers and landed proprietors." But Waterston's luck – and money – ran out in 1946. With no immediate prospect of employment in conservation, he went back to "the Firm" in Edinburgh. Geo. Waterston & Son welcomed back their prodigal son as sales director. Within a year, he was married and by 1950 was the father of a son.

* * *

John Buxton flew home in a Lancaster bomber:

> I kept wondering, during the flight from Rheims, whether, after more than five years without seeing her, I should recognise Marjorie when we met, perhaps in a crowd at a railway station, and whether she would recognise me. I knew that her hair had now some grey in it, and there must have been changes in my appearance, although I did not know what these were. "Mostly the look in your eyes," she said. My father made the same comment when he saw me a week later, and so did an old bookseller friend.

Buxton began a giddy round of visiting family and old friends:

> Soon we were asked out to dinner at the manor… I found the abundance of cutlery, after eating with a spoon out of a bowl for so long, perplexing, especially under the critical eye of a butler; and what, I tried to remember, did one do with asparagus?

Two days after his return, they went with a friend to count the birds at a heronry Marjorie had found during his absence. Soon they were at Buxton's parents in Cheshire, going to Redesmere, one of his favourite places. In his diary, he recorded reed warblers, willow warblers, chiffchaffs and whitethroats in song, peewits tumbling and crying, and great crested grebes and mallards on the water: "The hawthorn was in full flower and the bluebells and red campion just as before, but the countryside looking in better heart… better cared for and richer than before the war."

An apparently idyllic holiday in the Scilly Isles followed, watching seabirds, identifying flowers and fishing for mackerel from a small boat, but Marjorie's brother Ronald Lockley was deeply shocked by his brother-in-law's appearance when the couple went to stay with him in Pembrokeshire in July:

> He was a changed man… although he was as meticulous as ever in keeping records (as a naturalist)… the joy had gone out of his voice and looks, he would rarely open a conversation, though contributed to it intelligently when it was started. He was however unremittingly critical of almost everyone we knew, and had strange black moods which were very tough on my sister Marjorie. They frightened her.

Buxton went back to West Wales again in the summer of 1946, acting as volunteer warden on Skomer Island while he awaited demobilisation. At the end of that season on Skomer, he collapsed and was diagnosed as diabetic – a condition attributed to the treatment he had suffered as a POW. For the rest of his life, he was forced to inject himself with insulin daily. Embittered by what he saw as five wasted years, his health permanently compromised, Buxton had another reason for underlying unhappiness, one that he kept secret. His POW experience had rendered him sterile. Now the lines of a poem he had written in expectation five years before carried a dreadful weight:

And soon in peace our children shall be born
And we, together then, will watch them play.

John Buxton was to recoil from his inner turmoil by throwing himself into his work. But what would that be?

Promise fulfilled

"One has to make allowances for ex Prisoners of War."
Reverend Tom Griffiths, St Bride's Church, Dale,
Pembrokeshire (who knew Barrett, Buxton and
Conder well)

The men who had survived captivity and begun to accommodate to life in post-war Britain exhibited odd little foibles as a legacy of their experience. John Barrett could not bear to have anyone standing behind him when he was writing. He said it reminded him of Russian POWs who would lean over his shoulder, even though they could not read a word of his notes.

Even by birdwatchers' standards, Peter Conder was an obsessive recorder. At Minsmere nature reserve in Suffolk, he not only counted the avocets, he counted how many times each bird dipped its beak in the water. On RSPB official trips, he would ensure that delegates contributed to his bird list – a new one for every day.

John Buxton would never pass anything at the dinner table to anyone else – even to guests – but would determinedly help himself, as he had during five years of captivity, when prisoners scooped food into their mouths as fast as they could with their spoons.

Mild-mannered Barney Thompson would become irate if anyone asked where the prisoners had hidden "Jimmy" – the secret camp radio. He bluntly refused to disclose anything to anyone, even his close family, more than 65 years after the war had ended.

George Waterston had developed an aversion to a staple food of post-war Britain. "Don't pack those," Irene Waterston told a young assistant prior to an expedition. "George can't stand them – he said the Germans gave him nothing but baked beans."

* * *

By any except perhaps his own exacting standards, John Buxton's later career was a great success. At the beginning of 1940, he had written to his tutor Christopher Cox: "To have 3 potential lives (poet, don, naturalist) is all very well but one cannot make them all actual." At the end of the war he was in a not entirely dissimilar position. But what career should he choose? For months, as he agonised over his future life while awaiting demobilisation, he set about creating a legacy for his wartime efforts. There were papers to finalise for publication in the respected ornithological journals *British Birds* and the *Ibis* on migration, great tits and swallows. Most pressingly, Buxton, together with George Waterston, was keen to make the ideas about bird observatories that had developed in Eichstätt a working reality. The first meeting of the Bird Observatories Sub-Committee to coordinate work was held at Buxton's Buckinghamshire house. Buxton would sit on that committee, guiding the development of these important centres for bird conservation for the next sixteen years.

And then, of course, there were the redstarts. Just three days after the atomic bomb was dropped on Hiroshima, Buxton was struck by the incongruity of having a civilised lunch with Oxford ornithologists James Fisher, WB Alexander, HN Southern and David Lack, the newly appointed successor to Alexander as director of the Edward Grey Institute for Ornithology. Fisher stayed for dinner that evening and offered Buxton the chance to put his redstart findings in print as part of a new and expanding series of books published by Collins calledThe New Naturalists. *The Redstart* by John Buxton was published in 1950, one of the first bird monographs in an illustrious series that continues to this day. But by then, Buxton was lost to professional ornithology for good.

He had already decided on his path. Now in his mid-thirties, he ran through the options open to him, dismissing each in turn:

> More to my liking might have been a post as a professional ornithologist. But I had no academic qualifications for this – no degree in zoology or anything of the kind – and I did not wish to enter a career where I should always regard myself with suspicion as an amateur.

Instead of pursuing a further three years of unpaid study, Buxton wanted "a certain grace in living and in conversation, the quick responsive sympathy of cultivated minds, the quiet taste in everyday things – furniture, food, the garden – all these things, and clothes too; I have no intention of being deprived of such tokens of the quality of civilised life." Buxton's war years had furnished him with a literary CV, a body of well-received poetry. He accepted the offer of a paid English fellowship at Oxford's New College.

Buxton's career as a teacher and academic was not without its considerable highs. He became a lecturer, specialising in Elizabethan and seventeenth-century writing, producing books of characteristic breadth on Sir Phillip Sidney, Byron, Shelley and Elizabethan taste. Poet and lecturer in creative writing Andrew McNeillie remembers:

> His lectures were extraordinarily helpful. He had the gift of opening up his subject. He made Sidney's sonnet sequence "Astrophil and Stella" exciting and introduced his audience to others of the kind, notably I remember Fulke Greville's "Caelica". He seemed and was "old style" Oxford and a real scholar.

Buxton's material longings – a reaction to the privations he had suffered in war – were satisfied when he inherited a small fortune on his father's death and bought the Elizabethan moated manor house of Cole Park in Malmesbury. But Buxton never found real fulfilment. The poet who had blazed during the war had lost the inclination and confidence in his own ability to match, never mind surpass, what he had already written. He added very little to his poetry portfolio besides a paean to mark the wedding of Princess Elizabeth. His brother-in-law Ronald Lockley concurred with *The Times* obituarist (whom Lockley suspected to have been Iris Murdoch or another close friend), who would later write "In a German prison camp during that long captivity a poet had died and the books he was to write thereafter… were the works of a scholar, not the intense individual cry of a poet unable to keep silent."

Nor was he content in his role at Oxford:

I am by no means addicted to academic life – I prefer Scilly Islanders to dons, just as I was glad to have a chance to go to Norway in 1940 – yes, still in spite of 40–45. And I hate purely male society no doubt as a result of 5 years of it continuously. I ought to resign not later than 53–54 and there are times when I wonder if I can stand it so long.

Home life proved unsatisfactory too. Unable to give Marjorie the child she desperately wanted, Buxton refused her pleas to adopt. Marjorie showered affection on her nieces and nephews instead. His godson Murray Maclean remembered John as "aloof and distant", sitting alone in his study for hours at a time, a far cry from the pre-war young man who had carried Ronald Lockley's child on his shoulders. Buxton spent generously on wine and books for himself, but kept a tight hold on Marjorie's household expenditure. Lockley himself fell out with Buxton over what he saw as mean and cruel treatment of his sister.

There was a sense of what might have been in a letter Buxton wrote about meeting ornithologist James Fisher in Oxford on 16th October 1952:

One of the professional ornithologists here casually remarked that it was a pity I'd retired from that because work I did and got others doing during those years in Germany has led to two main developments since the war in field-work. This is, in fact, true; but I hadn't thought about it lately, as I knew I must give up when I came here. These two fields are the cooperative study either of a species or migration by a team of people; and the work of the bird observatories, which has pretty closely followed an article I sent home from prison, and which has been organised by a committee which I initiated... whose first meeting was held in my house.

But there was no going back. Ornithology at that time was modernising into a discipline that prioritised the dispassionate collection of data over the hitherto motley assimilation of random observations. Buxton, the meticulous gatherer of detail, displaying a thoroughly scientific approach, railed against what he saw as a reductive "professional" attitude in new ornithology and seemed to want to distance himself from it. *The Redstart* was a wonderful fusion of science and poetry that former Poet Laureate Andrew Motion called "a masterpiece" and a book that is still rated as one of the best bird monographs. But within its covers we see Buxton at open odds with his editors. In the introduction, James Fisher writes: "It is no longer, perhaps, advisable to attempt to distinguish in ornithology between the amateur and the professional. Technically speaking, John Buxton must be rated as an amateur, but he had done a most professional piece of work."

Buxton retorts:

If others can interpret my record more skillfully than I, then I shall be glad. Only I beg that they will go to look at the redstarts, till they know (as I know), that however much satisfaction there may be in tying up facts in neat parcels of theory, there is yet more in the mere observation. I have been content to record what we saw of the lives of these redstarts, which I love for their own sake, and not for the sake of adding to men's knowledge. I write as a naturalist and would here claim no other title.

For the rest of his life, Buxton pursued the life of a naturalist as a modest amateur on a smaller stage. His adopted county of Wiltshire benefited – he was a founder and council member of the Wildlife Trust and edited the *Birds of Wiltshire*. And he gave his university days friend Peter Scott advice on setting up his Gloucestershire centre for the Wildfowl & Wetlands Trust at Slimbridge. But after Marjorie died in 1977, he cut a sad and lonely figure. Robert Floyd of Chalfield Manor, whose family gave him company in his latter years, remembered him as "the most charming, diffident, erudite, wonderful person".

* * *

In 1947, the new acting assistant warden at Dale Fort in Pembrokeshire was doing his best to justify his appointment. In his own words, John Barrett was "no more than an old-fashioned, on-all-fours naturalist with no scientific, teaching or technical experience whatsoever". And here he was in charge of an outdoor education centre. Barrett was haunted by what he saw as a personal failure to engage other prisoners in natural history – "the chance was lost to show the beauty of simple things" and driven by a desire to make amends: "I intend to spend all next year on the flowers. I simply must know them more or less as I know birds," he told Barney Thompson. Barrett used the resourcefulness and make-do attitude he had learned in camp to render the decrepit buildings usable. Nails and wood came as flotsam and jetsam. The following year, the Fort took in its first students in residence under the tutelage of none other than Richard Purchon, Barrett's companion over many days of tree sparrow watching five years before.

For twenty years, students and schoolchildren came to stay at the Field Studies Centre under Barrett's supervision, a centre that gained an international reputation for teaching marine biology. The big, loud-voiced ex-RAF man terrified and then enchanted his students. His influence was enormous. Jim Atkinson, director of the University Marine Biological Station at Millport remembers:

I was in school doing A-level zoology and the class went to Dale Fort in Pembrokeshire in the summer of 1964. John welcomed us and entertained us with marine sagas before handing us over to one of his colleagues. John looked in on our progress as the week proceeded, and commented on our findings. He was firm yet genial and hugely knowledgeable. For me, that course at Dale was a career-forming turning point. A childhood of experiences messing round in rockpools suddenly made sense and fell into a logical framework.

Under his generous and loud exterior, Barrett could be a difficult employer and wartime hardships left him with low tolerance of other's discomforts and weaknesses: "A man is but a fool to complain of being cold in bed with his clothes on the chair

Barrett at the prow and Conder with his back to the camera, unloading a consignment of shearwaters (in the boxes marked URGENT) in June 1953. The birds were taken to Cambridge and released to test their homing powers. British Rail did not have "shearwater" on their list of approved livestock. They had "donkey", however, so Barrett labelled each box with the word DONKEY. All the birds returned before the message posted to say they had been released.

beside him," he often declared, and on walks he would race ahead, without ever pausing to let others catch up. Yet under his brusqueness, he was a loyal, kind man, and his friendship with his POW friends, Peter Conder in particular, endured.

For most naturalists, the name John Barrett is associated, if at all, with an indispensable book that they always took on holidays to the seaside. Published in 1958, the *Collins Guide to the Seashore* remained in print for nearly 40 years.

The names Barrett and Yonge appear on the cover, but it was Barrett who did the lion's share. Maurice Yonge, who had taught Barrett's fellow POW Richard Purchon at university before the war, did little more than lend his name to the title. Yonge admitted: "He is doing the bulk of the book; I have no time."

The "bulk" that Barrett took on occupied him for four years. Students collected specimens for the artists to draw and other students were the artists, for the publishers paid very little to have the illustrations drawn. Barrett stood over them, encouraging and pointing out tiny errors. He contacted naturalists in other parts of the UK, where he was less familiar with seashore life. The end result was universally lauded. Barrett's former colleague John Crothers commented that its influence "would be hard to exaggerate, both on the people who used it (one boy was heard to remark 'Sir, this animal is wrong'! [he trusted the book more than his own eyes]) and on a generation of authors/publishers who have sought to emulate it".

By 1968, Barrett saw himself at odds with what he saw as a restrictive, exam-fixated curriculum. Besides, he had recently begun a novel venture – leading organised guided walks. It distressed him that a million people visited Pembrokeshire every year, yet most went away afterwards with little under-standing of its natural treasures. He set up the Pembrokeshire Countryside Unit and began a walks and talks programme that was imitated throughout Britain. Except for visiting his children when they moved abroad, John Barrett never left Pembrokeshire. In retirement, accolades showered down on this remarkable, largely self-taught man: an MBE, an honorary MSc from the University of Wales, the 1989 National Park Award and perhaps most precious of all, the 1996 HH Bloomer Award from the Linnean Society for services to biology by an amateur biologist.

* * *

Peter Conder was still a withdrawn young man when he crossed the water to become the warden of Skokholm, now under the management of one John Barrett. His first summer was as a volunteer. The years thereafter were as a paid warden: "In addition to looking after visitors, my duties included the specific tasks of studying migration through Skokholm by keeping a daily record of the number of migrants and resident birds, by trapping, ringing, weighing, measuring them and removing their ectoparasites, and, of course, doing anything else conducive to the study, etc, etc — that standard catch-all phrase." Conder clearly found his additional duties more appealing: one member of a group from the RSPB's Junior Bird Recorders' Club remembered: "He was friendly to everyone who called, although you got the impression he was far happier with birds than people."

John Buxton advised him that he would have plenty of spare time that he could use fruitfully. Conder suggested he might study meadow pipits, but the wise head offered wheatears as an alternative – colourful, attractive birds, with the sexes easily

*Big shorts at Dale Fort: Barrett (right)
and Conder (left).*

distinguished. It was the same reasoning that had led Buxton
to pick redstarts all those years before.

Conder kept records fastidiously; they would come in handy
many years later. He used his time on the mainland produc-
tively too – wooing and marrying the island's supply officer
Pat Higginson in 1952. However, after their son was born,
the Conders realised that island life would be unsuitable for
a young family. In 1954, Conder took to the mainland and
accepted the first job he was offered, as assistant secretary at the
London-based RSPB.

It was a very different RSPB then, a tiny, rather ineffectual
organisation with just a few thousand members, a handful of
staff and precious few nature reserves. Conder became of necessity a jack-of-all-trades, traversing the country to deal with the
reserves, prosecutions and various nest protection schemes.

In 1963, the RSPB was thrown into disarray when the director Phillip Brown left suddenly. The Council decided that a quick succession was needed and, somewhat reluctantly, feeling they had little choice, appointed Peter Conder. Those working with him saw an astonishing transformation in this shy man who became energised and emboldened by responsibility. Research scientist Dr Gareth Thomas recalled: "He was responsible for taking the RSPB from rank amateurs to semi-professional. He started a division of labour, setting up the disciplines of reserves, education and, most importantly development. Membership went from 20,000 when he started to 200,000 when he retired."

One of his greatest achievements was leading voluntary organisations in a concerted campaign to bring about a ban on pesticides such as DDT, which had devastated countryside wildlife and virtually wiped out the peregrine and sparrowhawk.

Strangely, Conder's career had, in one significant respect, come full circle. Although there was no question about his bird knowledge, some senior conservation staff doubted his scientific ability. His greatest talents seemed to lie in the advertising, marketing and public relations fields that he thought he had left behind in 1946. Former colleagues remembered a man who was a PR dream, possessing a phenomenal memory for names and an uncanny ability to inspire: "He was the most charismatic conservationist I think I've ever met. He was a beautiful man; rugged features, a glint in his eye, a piratical gold tooth," remembered Dr Thomas.

By 1975, the selfless Conder, always putting the cause before his own personal ambition, had grown weary of life at the top. Troubled by coeliac disease that sapped his energy, and

Ruler of all he surveyed – Peter Conder at The Lodge.

struggling within an RSPB rocked by the effects of hyper-inflation, he had tired of his desk-bound, joyless job. He had seen one colleague step down from a senior office post to that of a reserve warden. Conder's own bolt-hole had been twice-yearly retreats with his family to the island of Alderney, but now it was his turn to escape for good. Thorough to the last, Conder hand-picked his successor in a government scientist called Ian Prestt and took "retirement" and an OBE at the relatively early age of 56. Buxton and Waterston worried about their overworked friend who now threw himself into the role of an international consultant and a committee man for organisations that included the National Trust, UNESCO, WWF and the then Nature Conservancy Council. His later years saw him wind down and follow the path set by his mentor. In 1989, weeks before the death of John Buxton, Conder published *The Wheatear*, the result of more than forty years of patient, methodical observation.

* * *

What of George Waterston? John Buxton noted: "George never found time to write up his wrynecks. Fine field naturalist though he was, George's talents were not for writing but rather for the practical tasks of organisation."

Waterston spent nine years back in the employ of the family firm, but it is unclear exactly how much time and effort was put into the printing and stationery business. He took long leaves of absence – four weeks at a time on Fair Isle, a week on bird observatory business with John Buxton, another couple of weeks on Fair Isle. And the office at the back of the Waterstons' shop became the Scottish Ornithologists' Club headquarters. Here Waterston was a slave to his typewriter, firing off letters to establish an observatory on his beloved island, seeking a runway, restoring a cottage, kicking at the post-war bureaucracy that demanded approval permits for everything down to a pot of paint. His relentless, obsessive drive bore fruit. On 8th January 1948, he informed John Buxton: "BIG NEWS! I am now proprietor of Fair Isle! I had to pay £3,000 eventually but feel it was well worth it… I hope to have the Observatory open in May when Ian Pitman and I go up for a fortnight."

A warden appointed, buildings renovated, Heligoland traps in place for ringing, the observatory opened that summer. Six years later, realising the necessity for outside sources of income to maintain the island's viability, the man people came to know as "the Laird of Fair Isle" sold it to the National Trust for Scotland for the same amount he had paid.

Somewhere he left his first wife Nancy in his wake and had little contact thereafter with his son William, who was just two years old when the couple separated. The reality was that George was married to birds. His second wife Irene, an SOC committee member, dovetailed interests with her workaholic husband and was a significant and much-underrated driving force behind his work.

In January 1955, Waterston took a financial gamble. The RSPB offered him part-time work as its representative in Scotland. At the same time, the SOC agreed to pay a part-time salary to the man who had been its unpaid secretary since 1936. Waterston left "the Firm" and ruled his dual empire from

The Laird of Fair Isle. The owner pictured some time after the island's purchase in 1948.

a single room in the National Trust for Scotland's Edinburgh headquarters until 1959, when the RSPB made him its full-time representative and later director for Scotland.

Waterston was not one for petty territoriality. The organisations he worked for were simply a means to an end. While he was the RSPB's director in Scotland, he was a founder of the Scottish Wildlife Trust and remained active elsewhere in conservation. A junior colleague, Mike Everett, remembered that, in the 1960s: "Seventy-five per cent of your time would be spent on RSPB business, then you'd suddenly be called on to do something for the SOC or Fair Isle. I doubt Peter Conder would have worried – George probably did more hours for the RSPB than anyone else. Office was home for George – he lived upstairs and would go up for tea then come down and rattle away on his typewriter, fag in his mouth, until midnight."

On his many visits south to the RSPB's Bedfordshire headquarters at The Lodge, Waterston and his wife Irene invariably stayed with the Conders and a deeper friendship developed between the two very different men.

Impeccably connected, endlessly energetic, a recipient of an OBE in 1964 for services to British ornithology and conservation, Waterston masterminded the expansion of the RSPB in Scotland. New reserves were secured on Shetland and Orkney and at Lochwinnoch, Loch Garten, Vane Farm on Loch Leven, and Balranald in the Outer Hebrides. Visiting the far-flung outposts of his empire in an ancient dormobile, he would emerge, the down-at-heel scion of one of Scotland's most famous families, dressed in an old tweed suit and plus fours with patched knees.

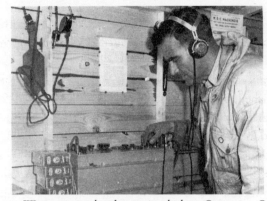

*Above: Waterston in the observation hide at Operation Osprey
listening to the sounds of young ospreys in the nest.
Below (right to left): Waterston, Johan Willgohs and warden Roy
Dennis at the introduction of four Norwegian white-tailed eaglets
on Fair Isle in 1968. Though the birds failed to breed, a further
reintroduction seven years later on Rum proved successful.*

But Waterston was best known at the RSPB for setting up Operation Osprey on Speyside. Stuffed specimens of the bird that had become extinct in Scotland before he was even born had entranced him as a boy. It was his dream to see the birds re-established, so when nesting attempts in the mid-1950s at Loch Garten were thwarted by egg collectors, he supervised a protection scheme, instigating a round-the-clock watch and surrounding the nest tree with barbed wire. Though to modern eyes it seems an echo of Waterson's POW camp experience, the Fair Isle warden of the 1950s, Peter Davis, put it in historical perspective: "In those days, there was barbed wire everywhere: if you wanted to keep people out, you put it up."

This was a military exercise and Waterston planned the operation with military precision. He rattled out a STRICTLY CONFIDENTIAL document declaring: "The greatest possible secrecy will be observed while the birds are incubating their eggs. G.W., with the aid of voluntary observers, will keep close watch against any trespassers and any other form of disturbance." It was at this point that Waterston came up with what the then RSPB director Phillip Brown called "one of the most scatter-brained notions that I had ever heard". Waterston suggested inviting the public to come and watch. That first controlled public nestwatch scheme, guiding people to where they could be tolerated without causing harm, and away from where they could not, has been the most popular of all, attracting more than two million visitors.

Though Waterston's drive never left him, his health did. By the early 1970s, the first signs of renal failure were evident and in 1972, he took early retirement. Kidney transplant operations in 1975 failed and were followed by dialysis, which he endured without complaint. A portable dialysis machine accompanied him to Fair Isle in July 1980. Two months later, on 20th September, George Waterston died at the age of 69. Robert Waterston lost "an inspirational big brother" and conservation lost a slightly built giant. His name lives on: the Scottish Ornithologist's Club centre on the Firth of Forth was named Waterston House in his honour, and on his beloved Fair Isle stands the George Waterston Memorial Centre.

MEMORIES

More than fifteen years after his death in 1993, Peter Conder's daughter Sarah began, for the first time, to properly read and type up the letters her father had sent home from his POW camps. It prompted her to go into the attic to fish out something from among his belongings: an old-style, saucer-sized floppy disk labelled "Memoirs". Another year passed before she found a software engineer who was able to decode the contents. The disk contained a file titled "Birdwatching POWs". It tantalised and frustrated, ending abruptly after just seven and a half pages in March 1942 with the line: "Several of these diving rooks materialised out of the blue sky diving and gliding towards the piles of manure." At that point, a quest began to piece together the full story of Peter Conder and his birdwatching companions.

Most of the men who returned from their POW camps in 1945 were in no hurry to tell their tales. For years, Barney Thompson was haunted by images of being inside a burning plane. "Don't talk about the war," his wife would warn their daughters; "it will only bring back his nightmares." Peter Conder's instinct was to blot the war out of his life. A man who worked a great deal with Conder was fellow POW Norman

Moore, who had watched black redstarts from his hospital bed in a Polish camp towards the end of the war. Moore, a scientific officer with the then Nature Conservancy Council and a world authority on dragonflies, said: "Some people talked about the war, some didn't. Peter didn't." In 1993, when he knew he was dying, Conder told his sister Natalie: "I was so glad you never mentioned it." Perhaps the most traumatised of them all, John Buxton said nothing to anyone for many years and it was made quite clear to his nieces and nephews that the topic was out of bounds.

Other prisoners who might have been prepared to speak shared the sense of disconnection felt by Buxton's fellow librarian at Eichstätt, Dorrien Belson: "It became abundantly clear very early on that anything to do with my war experiences during the last five years was a taboo subject and it was indeed studiously avoided by everyone I met and even within family. I felt at times rather akin to someone who had recently been bereaved." That disconnection, the buttoned-up stiff upper lip that so many would mention, worked both ways – most of their contemporaries had fought through the war and lived through horrors of their own. In the aftermath of war, most of them maintained a conspiracy of silence, hoping to seal that part of their life up. Vincent Hollom's younger brother Jasper (a fellow veteran of Eichstätt) summed up a prevailing mood of dismissive pragmatism: "One's eyes were fixed on what one would do next." These were young men – some approaching middle age – who wanted to make up for lost opportunities and forge a life ahead.

Perhaps by the 1970s and 80s, the past was indeed another country for these men, whose emotional wounds had begun to heal or at least fade. The rush of derring-do escape films and books in the 1950s – *The Wooden Horse* and *The Colditz Story* – passed them by as largely irrelevant to their experiences. But in later years, *The Great Escape* and the BBC series *Colditz* glamorised POW life, and ex-servicemen began to be caught up in a new desire to record their stories.

The birdwatchers now had a new generation of naïve and curious relations, friends and workmates. George Waterston kept his war notebooks on a shelf by his desk and freely left them available to a younger colleague whose own father had fought in the war. He would recount his experiences too… but only if asked. On his retirement, Peter Conder put a sense of obligation before personal reticence when asked to write an article for the RSPB's junior magazine about what it was like to be a POW birdwatcher. John Barrett, the born storyteller, was, in the right circumstances, more forthcoming, regaling Barney Thompson's war-mad grandson with stories of his life in the RAF. But there were private, painful areas where he would not go. Before dementia took away his brilliant, inventive mind in the 1990s, he wrote a biography, circulated privately, which revealed an astonishing recall of events that had taken place half a century before, but one that side-stepped personal disclosures.

John Buxton remained an enigma to the end. In the last year of his life, this deeply shy man, who was only ever truly comfortable among others in formal situations, poured all his eloquence out with his pen one last time in a memoir of his war years. Writing was always the one thing that he could control and order. Buxton sought to have the memoir published, but had a rejection. There was no time to try again – a misunderstanding over his diabetic medication led to his sudden death in 1989 at the age of 76. A condition brought on by captivity had denied him the opportunity to manage its legacy.

The four men who shared watches on the mudheap of Warburg and in the valley of Eichstätt had remained friends for the rest of their lives. An impassioned Barrett was firm in his belief that their wartime experience had created a special bond between them: "Pre-war friendships between some of us welded all four into the closest association. None of our succeeding trials ever threatened to shake us apart. Never. Our unity was intimate."

* * *

We should conclude, not with these birds in a cage, but at a happier point when they were at or near the peak of their professional lives. In the summer of 1960, surrounded by his wife and children, John Barrett stayed put in his Pembrokeshire domain, as he did every summer. "Living in a place like that, why would we want to go on holiday anywhere else?" asked his youngest son Rob. At Operation Osprey on the RSPB reserve at Loch Garten, George and Irene Waterston hosted some very special visitors, Irene's practical ying offsetting George's mercurial yang. On a busman's holiday, Peter and Pat Conder had brought their two little children, who were given a caravan to themselves. John and Marjorie Buxton arrived too, with John, one step removed from direct social engagement, acting as photographer. Every night, *lichts aus* (lights out) came when each of them decided. Every morning they woke without guards rapping at their doors, bursting in uninvited to shout "*Raus,*

raus!" And then they would go outside in their own time with their wives and families to look for birds wherever they wanted, and enjoy a certain kind of pleasure in freedom that none of us can possibly understand.

Derek Niemann is the editor of the RSPB's children's magazines and has written several books on nature and conservation for young readers. He lives in Bedfordshire with his family.

BIBLIOGRAPHY

Barrett, John, "Some notes on the breeding habits of the chaffinch" (*Ibis* 89, 1947)

Barrett, John, Conder, Peter, and Thompson, AJB, "Some notes on the crested lark" (*British Birds* XLI, 1947)

Barrett, John, "Some of my days" (unpublished memoir, c1993)

Beckwith, Captain EGC (editor), *The Quill: A Collection of Prose, Verse and Sketches by Officers Prisoner-of-War in Germany, 1940-1945* (Country Life Books, 1950)

Belson, Dorrien, *Caught: Prisoner of War No. 487* (AuthorHouse, 2008)

Brown, Philip, *Scottish Ospreys: from Extinction to Survival* (Heinemann, 1979)

Buxton, John "The breeding of the oyster-catcher" (*British Birds* XXXIII, 1939)

Buxton, John, *Westward* (Jonathan Cape, 1942)

Buxton, John, *Such Liberty* (Macmillan & Co, 1944)

Buxton, John, *Atropos and Other Poems* (Macmillan & Co, 1946)

Buxton, John, *The Redstart* (Collins, 1950)

Buxton, John, "Migration of birds observed in NW Germany 1942" (*Ibis* 95, 1953)

Buxton, John, "The end of a war" (unpublished memoir, 1989)

Cochrane, AL, "Notes on the psychology of prisoners of war" (*British Medical Journal*, 23 February 1946)

Conder, Peter, "The breeding biology and behaviour of the continental goldfinch *Carduelis carduelis carduelis*" (*Ibis* 90, 1948)

Conder, Peter, "Individual distance" (*Ibis* 91, 1949)

Conder, Peter, "Bird watching" (RSPB *Bird Life*, 1985)

Conder, Peter, *The Wheatear* (Christopher Helm, 1989)

Crothers, John, "Obituary: JH Barrett" (*Field Studies* 9, 2000)

Dearlove, AR, "Enforced leisure: a study of the activities of officer prisoners of war" (*British Medical Journal*, 24 March 1945)

Fisher, James, *Watching Birds* (Penguin, 1940)

Forrester R, Andrews I, et al, *The Birds of Scotland* (Scottish Ornithologists' Club, 2007)

Gilbert, Adrian, *POW: Allied Prisoners in Europe 1939-1945* (John Murray, 2006)

Gilbert, Martin, *The Second World War: a Complete History* (Weidenfeld & Nicolson, 1989, reprint Phoenix, 2009)

Innes, Bill (editor), *St-Valery: the Impossible Odds* (Birlinn, 2004)

James, David, *A Prisoner's Progress* (William Blackwood, 1947)

Johnson, Kristin, "A naturalist in wartime: John Buxton's pioneering study of the redstart" (*The Naturalist* 135, 2010)

Kee, Robert, *A Crowd is Not Company* (Eyre & Spottiswoode, 1947)

Longden, Sean, *Dunkirk: the Men they Left Behind* (Constable, 2009)

Lockley, RM, *Letters from Skokholm* (JM Dent & Sons, 1947, reprint Little Toller Books, 2010)

Maclean, Murray, *Five Years to Liberty: the War Poems of John Buxton 1940-45* (Pentland Press, 1994)

Moore, PG, "Illustrations and the genesis of Barrett and Yonge's Collins pocket guide to the sea shore" (1958) (*Archives of natural history* 37.2 (2010) Edinburgh University Press)

Morrell, Stephen, *Scattering Dreams: a History of Dale Fort* (Field Studies Council, 2011)

Nichol, John and Rennell, Tony, *The Last Escape: the Untold Story of Allied Prisoners of War in Germany 1944-45* (Viking, 2002)

Nicholson, EM, *The Art of Birdwatching* (HF & G Witherby, 1931)

Niethammer, Günther, *Beobachtungen über die Vogelwelt von Auschwitz* (Naturhistorisches Museum Wien, 1942)

Nowak, Eugeniusz, "Erinnerungen an frühere ornithologen" (*Journal für Ornithologie* 139, 1998)

Pennie, Ian Durance, Obituary: George Waterston OBE, LL D, FRSE (*Scottish Birds* 11, 1980)

Purchon, Richard, *The Nesting Activities of the Swallow* (Proceedings of the Zoological Society, 1948)

Prittie, TCF, and Edwards, W Earle, *Escape to Freedom* (Hutchinson, 1946)

Rollings, Charles, *Wire and Worse: RAF Prisoners of War in Laufen, Biberach, Lübeck and Warburg 1940-42* (Ian Allan, 2004)

Rollings, Charles, *Prisoner of War: Voices from Behind the Wire in the Second World War* (Ebury Press, 2008)

Scott, Peter, *The Eye of the Wind: an Autobiography* (Hodder & Stoughton, 1961)

Stresemann, Erwin, "Die Vögel Kretas" (*Journal für Ornithologie* 91, 1943)

Thom, Valerie M, *Fair Isle: an Island Saga* (John Donald, 1989)

Walker, David, *Lean, Wind, Lean: a Few Times Remembered* (Collins, 1985)

Wartime memories project (www.wartimememories.co.uk)

Waterhouse, "MJ, Rook and Jackdaw Migrations Observed in Germany, 1942-1945" (*Ibis* 91, 1949)

Williams, Eric, *The Wooden Horse: the Greatest Escape Story of World War II* (Fontana, 1949)

Wood, JER (editor), *Detour: the Story of Oflag IVC* (Falcon Press, 1946)

Wynn, Richard, "A Fighter Pilot's Diary of World War 2" (unpublished memoir, 2001)

ACKNOWLEDGEMENTS

Six weeks after he shared his memories of messmate "Birdie" Conder, Lt Col Ernest Edlmann passed away in his sleep. It was his 98th birthday. The last living link – as far as I know – with the four birdwatchers of Warburg has gone.

Nevertheless, the men in those POW camps have been brought back to us thanks to the families, friends and colleagues who – without exception – have given their support to this book. First and foremost, I owe a huge, admiring debt to Sarah Rhodes (née Conder), who has kept a fire burning for her father throughout with tireless research and a giving heart. Her husband David has given wise advice and her mother, Pat Conder (née Higginson), has offered telling comments, both about her late husband and his companions. Peter's "darling sis", Natalie Oliver, recounted pre-war tales of her brother to me and we are fortunate that Peter's son David Conder had a child's curiosity and a good memory. Thanks also to Susan Conder for allowing us access to her husband Neville's correspondence.

John Buxton's nephew and godson Murray Maclean was extremely helpful. We are indebted also to his niece Philippa Home who gave permission to reproduce Buxton's remarkable poems. Rob Barrett in northern Norway was a great advocate for his father and spokesman for his siblings, Tiggy Davies and Ann Mark helped with contacts. Robert Waterston added unique insights into his big brother's wartime experience and William and Andrea Waterston gave their welcome blessing to use of his writing.

The heartrending story of "Barney" Thompson would not have appeared at all had it not been for his daughter Jan, who shares his impish sense of humour and gave so much of his writing and her time. Thanks also to her husband Tony Pickup for his willing assistance. Peter Conder gave Tony his first job at the RSPB. What goes around, comes around…

The relatives of the men's comrades helped build a bigger picture or gave permission for their soldier forebears' work to be reproduced here. Many thanks to Nigel Purchon, Andrea Wheeler (née Hollom), her cousin Diana Summers, Giles Munby, Tessa Howard (née Edlmann), and the children of George Raeburn. Friends and former colleagues brought colour. Mike Everett, a great observer of character, was especially valuable with his entertaining recollections of George Waterston, who said little and wrote less. Telling insights also came from Gareth Thomas, Frank and Kathleen Hamilton, Nick Hammond, Peter Davis, David Saunders, Steve Morrell, Mary Thomas, John Say, John Price, Robert Floyd, Jim Atkinson, Geoff Moore, Andrew McNeillie, Jim Perrin and Maimie Nethersole-Thompson.

Ex POWs Sir Jasper Hollom and Norman Moore offered gripping first-hand accounts of their war experiences. Bjorn Ulf Noll and Peter Green boosted our knowledge of the Rotenburg period, Norbert Schäffer found information on German ornithologists, Alex Cox gave a psychologist's insight to the men's behaviour.

No book of this nature would be possible without custodians of the written word. Special thanks to Fair Islander Anne Sinclair of the George Waterston Memorial Centre and Museum, Rod Suddaby and staff at the Imperial War Museum, RSPB librarian Elizabeth Allen, who loaned me more books than I deserved, Sophie Wilcox at the Alexander Library of Ornithology (bribed with buns!), Karen Bidgood, John Savory, Ian Elfick, Keith Macgregor, Catherine Cant and Wendy Hicks at the SOC's beautiful Waterston House library overlooking Aberlady Bay (more buns), Jennifer Thorp at Oxford's New College and Colin Harris and his staff at the Special Collections of the Bodleian Library.

ACKNOWLEDGEMENTS

Many people guided this book into production. Mark Cocker coined the title and generously passed on the opportunity to write it. Rob Hume used his considerable artistic skills and ornithological knowledge to produce so many illustrations with an authentic feel. Modest Helen Macdonald shared the trail and gave willingly of her research while she wrote her excellent BBC radio drama on the same subject, *Through the Wire*. RSPB colleagues offering support and indulgence included Mark Boyd, Kate Smith, Mike Hopwood, Janet Pedley, Sheila Abrams and Guy Anderson. Midge Gillies and Simon Barnes both gave morale-boosting breaks. Children's fiction writer Lucy Christopher offered perceptive comments on the first draft. And of course, Aurea Carpenter and Rebecca Nicolson at Short Books had the faith and imagination to believe in a story that needed telling. Thanks to Aurea in particular for making this such a joyful and painless experience.

Finally, no undertaking of this size could be completed without the support of the author's family. Thanks to my son Mike for his encouragement and insight, and to my ever-patient wife Sarah, who has given so much and shown great forbearance when my body was here, but my head was behind the wire.

Index